History *of* Lexington Conference

History *of* Lexington Conference

DAVID. E. SKELTON

COMMONWEALTH BOOK COMPANY
ST. MARTIN, OHIO

Copyright © 1950 by David. E. Skelton
Originally published by History of Lexington Conference
This edition copyright © 2024 by Commonwealth Book Company

All rights reserved. No part of this book may be reproduced in any form or by any means without the prior written consent of the publisher, excepting brief quotes used in reviews.
Printed in the United States of America.

ISBN: 978-1-948986-74-8

COVER IMAGE: METHODIST CHURCH, ELKIN NORTH CAROLINA
LIBRARY OF CONGRESS, PRINTS & PHOTOGRAPHS DIVISION
GOTTSCHO-SCHLEISNER COLLECTION

Contents

Preface	5
Introduction to Conference History	7
Authors	12
Commendations by Friends of the Conference	13
College of Bishops—Central Jurisdiction	20
Historical Sessions of the Conference	30
Unsung Heroes	32
Presiding Elders and District Superintendents, 1869-1946	35
Chronological Roll	38
The First Race Man to Hold Our Conference	39
The Church Women's Work	41
Laymen's Work	46
Statistical Review	51
Delegates to the General and Jurisdictional Conference	58
Preacher's Relief Association	61
Secretaries of the Conference	63
Treasurers of the Conference	64
Miscellaneous Items	65

DR. D. E. SKELTON   MRS. D. E. SKELTON

Preface

This volume does not discuss people who were gifted in craftsmanship, architecture, masonry, nor art. Just fifteen men called of God to preach His gospel to a lost world, and go forth to build the Kingdom of God among men.

What has been done in so short a time is remarkable. Fifteen ministers, all of whom were slaves, should lay a foundation upon which we have built with 1,500 members in 1870 and now 39,000 in 1947.

In 1870 these unlettered men went forth to build Christianity in the lives of those who by the Emancipation had come into a new world. Before them was the granite of opportunity. 4,560,000 slaves who were given their freedom with not a foot of land they could call their own. Yet with the chisel of faith and the mallet of an unconquered will power, they began to carve an image that will last through eternity. An image like unto Him who said, "I came not to save those who were saved, but those who are to be saved." So as you read this little volume, may it give you an inspiration to work.

This book is dedicated to my wife, Georgia Morton, who for sixty years has stood by me in sorrow and joy.

DAVID E. SKELTON

Introduction to Conference History

Having been born in Kentucky, having known the organizers of the Conference personally, and having labored in the Conference as pastor, Presiding Elder and District Superintendent for more than sixty years, Doctor David E. Skelton is eminently fitted for the task of writing the Conference history.

Since he has brought more preachers into the Conference than any other two men combined, he is rightfully called the Father of the Conference. Add to these men brought into the Conference by those whom he brought and the many fine laymen who are products of his preaching the gospel of Christ and you have a picture of his standing in the Conference.

It is important that we have such an historic record now while there are living witnesses of those early beginnings. Others may re-write in later years but must have these facts here recorded by Dr. D. E. Skelton which show not only the men who labored but also the conditions under which they labored, in order that proper evaluations might be made.

Let every minister and every up-to-date layman place a copy in his own library.

B. F. SMITH

HISTORY OF THE LEXINGTON CONFERENCE
By Dr. Jos. Courtney, *P. E. Louisville District*

The Lexington Annual Conference of the Methodist Episcopal Church was originally a part of the Kentucky Annual Conference of the Methodist Episcopal Church.

At the session of the Kentucky Annual Conference of the Methodist Episcopal Church at Covington, Ky., in the spring of 1866, several Negro preachers were admitted on trial into the traveling connection. This body met as one body for three consecutive years, during which others were admitted. At the annual session held in Newport, Ky., in 1868, the Negro preachers expressed a desire that a new Annual Conference might be formed, to be composed of themselves, at as early a period as practicable. The Kentucky Conference, after hearing the desire as it had been expressed by its Negro members, adopted a resolution asking the General Conference, which met the same year, 1868, to provide for the wishes of its Negro members. The action of the General Conference was favorable to their wishes.

At the session of the Kentucky Conference held at Harrodsburg, Ky., in the spring of 1869, Bishop Levi Scott presiding, the new Conference was organized, March 2, 1869. The name adopted for it was that which it now bears, the "Lexington Conference."

The original members of the Conference, when organized, are as follows: namely, Hanson Talbott, H. H. Lytle, George W. Downing, Nelson Sanders, Andrew Bryant, W. L. Muir, E. C. Moore, Zale Ross, and W. H. Lawrence.

Thus these fathers, with all of their incompetency, did the pioneer work and laid the foundation of this great Conference. They were not anxious about positions of honor, but what they demanded were places where they could work for God and humanity.

Oh, my, how they were blessed in their work, and how the Church did prosper under their administration in those days! The growth of this Conference in the last thirty-four years, numerically and intellectually, has been marvelous. It has among its members several graduates from reputable schools; several who have been honored with honorary degrees.

I believe I am justified in saying that this Conference has, upon the whole, as able corps of ministers as any Negro conference in the Church. The lay members have stood for several years about one thing. This is caused by the constant drainage made upon the churches in Kentucky, by hundreds of the members moving into the Middle and Northwestern States. The revivals and the increase in the membership annually are about equal to the number that moves out from us.

In 1873 the white conference in Ohio turned over to our Conference all the colored work in Ohio. In this turnover we came into possession of the following work: Mt. Healthy, College Hill, Cummingsville, Oberlin, Dayton, Springfield, Cleaves, Cincinnati. These churches

HISTORY OF THE LEXINGTON CONFERENCE

were added to those coming from the Washington Conference, and a new district was added, namely the Ohio, with W. C. Echols the presiding elder.

The Conference now had four districts: the Bowling Green, Henry Lytle, presiding elder; the Lexington with David P. Jones, presiding elder; the Louisville with W. L. Muir, presiding elder; the Ohio with W. C. Echols, presiding elder. With this increase the Conference was still too small to be more than a mission conference. With the coming in of the Class of 1873 composed of Jos. Courtney, Geo. Board, John Norris, D. W. Heston, Henry W. Johnson, James Taylor, George Leach, Albert W. Price, and A. W. Skinner in 1876, the Conference became a conference rather than a mission conference.

In 1875 the Indiana District was organized. Connersville, Jeffersonville, Shelbyville, Rockport, Browns, Ill., Graysville, Ill., had churches, and there were missions at Anderson, Ind., Lawrenceville, Ill., Marion, Ill., with Madison and North Vernon as a circuit. Connersville and Shelbyville were the largest appointments at this time. W. L. Muir was made presiding elder of this work.

In 1876 W. L. Muir and Geo. W. Sissle were elected delegates to the General Conference which met in Baltimore and they succeeded in changing the status of the Conference to an Annual Conference.

The following men were considered as leaders of the Conference at that time: W. L. Muir, Daniel Jones, Marshall W. Taylor, E. W. S. Hammond, Geo. A. Sissle, Joseph Courtney, Henderson Talbert.

The early scholars of the church were: Daniel Jones, W. C. Echols, Marshall W. Taylor, John F. Mooreland, Sr., and E. W. S. Hammond.

The great preachers in the early history were: Geo. W. Downing, E. W. S. Hammond, Marshall W. Taylor, W. W. Locke, Abraham Booker, Felix Ross, Thos. Thompson, Paris Fisher, Geo. A. Sissle, Marcus McCoomer, Scott Ward, Frank Hinton, J. W. Mooreland, Sr., J. S. Johnson, and T. L. Ferguson. To these must be given the credit for what the Lexington Conference is today.

HISTORY OF THE LEXINGTON CONFERENCE

By W. L. MUIR

The organization of the Lexington Conference Mission was held in Harrodsburg, Ky., at the session of the Kentucky Conference (white). To this Mission Conference was given 1,500 members, 11 churches, 10 ordained ministers. The ordained ministers were: David P. Jones, W. L. Muir, Henry Lytle, Nathaniel L. Carr, Mammoth Walton, C. T. Jones, Gale Ross, Israel Simms, George W. Downing, and Nelson Saunders. At this session there were the following unordained ministers: Zacharia Winchester, Joseph L. Gobel, Felix Ross, Paris Fisher, Adam Nunn, Henry W. White, Henry Gibson, Daniel Tucker, and Elijah Henderson. These nineteen men began the building of the Lexington Conference. To these men we owe a lasting debt of gratitude for their faith, courage and loyalty as pioneers of our Methodism.

From eleven church buildings, we have today, 137 church buildings. In 1869 we had 19 ministers and today we have 122 effective ministers, 16 retired ministers, 34 supply pastors and 4 supernumerary ministers. Including supply pastors, we have 146 ministers and a total of 160 ministers with a membership of 28,338. The value of our church property is $2,051,550. We have parsonage property valued at $241,115.

The organization of the Lexington Conference was completed in 1869, and at this time two districts were set up with the Lexington District having 12 preaching places, and the Louisville District having 16 preaching places. Henry Lytle was appointed presiding elder of the Louisville District. D. P. Jones was placed at the head of the Lexington District. The salaries of the superintendents were $600 a year. Many of the ministers were sent to appointments where we had neither churches or memberships. These men went out from Harrodsburg with but one thought to build the Kingdom of God. They built no stately brick structures such as we have now, but they did build in the lives of men Christian character which will stand after brick and mortar shall have crumbled away.

HISTORY OF THE LEXINGTON CONFERENCE

In 1871 Zachariah Winchester, Jas. L. Gobel, Felix Ross, Paris Fisher, Adam Nunn, Henry White, Daniel Tucker, Henry Gibson, Elijah Henderson were admitted on trial. In 1871 the Bowling Green District was made with 17 preaching places with Henderson Tolbert as the presiding elder. In 1872 W. L. Muir was elected the first delegate to the General Conference held in New York City. It was at this conference that he had the boundary line of the Conference to include Ohio, Kentucky, Indiana, and Illinois east of the Illinois Railroad. This boundary brought to us from the Washington Conference: Cadiz, Bellaire, Bridgeport, Flushing, Georgetown, Mt. Pleasant, Ohio, Martins Ferry, Steubenville, Zanesville. From the Washington Conference came the following ministers: W. C. Echols, E. W. S. Hammond, John H. Mooreland, A. W. Hargraves, Armstead, Skinner, K. D. Williams, and W. C. Statesman, as a supply minister.

Authors

Dr. Marshall W. Taylor published *The Plantation Melodies*.

Dr. Louis M. Hagood published the book, *The Negro in the Methodist Episcopal Church*.

In 1909 Dr. Walter H. Riley published the book, *Forty Years in the Lap of Methodism*.

We now give you a brief history of the achievements of the last forty years.

Commendations by Friends of the Conference

Ecumenical Methodist Council
WESTERN SECTION

Winter Home
Randolph Hotel
St. Petersburg, Fla.
February 27, 1946

The Rev. David E. Skelton, D.D.
321 West 29th St.
Indianapolis

Dear Dr. Skelton:

It interests me to hear again from Lexington Conference, which I came to know rather well in the days when Methodist bishops were really General Superintendents.

The incident you describe and which, with comments on the Conference in general, you wish me to relate for the history of the body which you are preparing, *needs a little fuller statement.* In 1913, seven years before the Lexington Conference was placed in the Indianapolis Area under my administration, I had not been assigned by the Episcopal Committee to preside at its session. That appointment had been given to one of the bishops in the East. When the big flood came he did not like the look of a trip to Louisville and kept waiting for an all-clear weather signal. None came. So he wired me that the Conference could not ordain its men or make legal appointments. He asked me to go and attend to the business. My family objected. They thought, and truly, that the floods were no easier to encounter from the south than from the east and that the trip from Atlanta was dangerous. My reply was, "Those men cannot be left like that. Someone must go, and at once. They have been waiting too long now." There was plenty of water, but I arrived as dry as a preacher needs to be. It was not the *first* of April, but the second, according to my minute. The session was no April fool affair, and I did not treat it like one. While the members sang and prayed, I went over with the Cabinet everything that had been done and all the appointments proposed. Then I spoke to the Conference on "The Prophet for the Twentieth Century," ordained elders, took up the list of appointments and said, in substance, "Dr. Courtney and the members of the Cabinet have done a careful and excellent piece of work, and I shall read the assignments just as they appear on this paper." I gave the men a few words of counsel and of good wishes, and we stood adjourned.

HISTORY OF THE LEXINGTON CONFERENCE

After the Lexington Conference was made a part of the Indianapolis Area I presided in three out of four years of the quadrennium. The three sessions when I was present were in Cleveland, April 20-24, 1921; Covington, Ky., April 19-23, 1922; and Louisville, Ky., April 9-13, 1924. At all of these Conferences I spoke daily and preached Sundays. At Cleveland I gave a lecture on "The Philosophy of a Happy Life." J. B. Redmond was pastor in Cleveland and J. H. Ross in Covington. In the latter place we had our great missionary hero, Bishop Hartzell, with us and he spoke on "The Will of God."

On looking the matter up I find that the Conference of 1923 was held in my home city, Indianapolis, under the presidency of Bishop Jones. At the latter's request I presided in one session and took part in the Sunday morning service at Simpson Church, W. J. White, pastor.

My recollection is that during the quadrennium in which I was related to it so closely Lexington Conference never had a trial for any serious offence. I am sure that no unpleasant episode occurred in any of the meetings held. I was not able of course to travel widely through a Conference covering so large a territory and extending into ten states of the Union, but I responded to requests for addresses and sermons, as well as other work, when I could do so. All of the Conferences of Indiana were also in my field of duty.

I recall a good many men of the Conference. Besides those already named I well remember the Conference officials, W. H. Riley and S. H. Sweeney, now of New York, and with these men, G. R. Bryant, E. A. White, H. M. Carroll, J. W. Robinson, W. P. Kellogg and D. E. Skelton. I could name more, some of whom wrought well and have long since gone to their reward.

The history of Lexington Conference is well worth gathering up and preserving. I have often thought and said that they who have no regard for history will make little history. Personally, I am now at work collecting the oldest *Disciplines* and histories of American Methodism, as well as the letters and manuscripts of the early bishops and leaders of the Church. These documents, which I have assembled in large quantities, will be of great use on the part of future biographers and historians.

With Christian greetings to you and to the Conference, and with all good wishes.

Very sincerely,
FREDERICK D. LEETE

Illinois Wesleyan University
BLOOMINGTON, ILLINOIS
Office of the President

WILLIAM E. SHAW

February 27, 1946

It has been my pleasure to know Dr. David E. Skelton since we were boys together at Moore's Hill, Indiana.

Because of this early acquaintance I have been unusually interested to know of the place of leadership he has occupied in the Lexington Conference and in the wider circles of The Methodist Church. Having been so closely related to the work of the Lexington Conference for many years, he is unusually well fitted to write its history.

W. E. SHAW
President

HISTORY OF THE LEXINGTON CONFERENCE

Division of Home Missions and Church Extension of the Board of Missions and Church Extension of The Methodist Church

1701 ARCH STREET   PHILADELPHIA 3, PA.

SECTION OF CHURCH EXTENSION

March 13, 1946

Dr. David E. Skelton
321 W. 29th Street
Indianapolis, Indiana

Dear Dr. Skelton:

In my 25 years of service in the field of Church Extension I have had the privilege of contact with the 19 Negro Conferences of The Methodist Church and getting acquainted with a large part of its personnel. While the needs and many perilous conditions of this part of the work, especially in the distressful period of the decade of economic depression, caused much anxiety, I nevertheless greatly enjoyed the cooperation with the Bishops, District Superintendents, pastors and laymen of these Conferences. Among these associations I count as most interesting and delightful my contact with District Superintendent and pastor David E. Skelton. His unique manner of approach in representing the individual church's needs and in applying for consideration, his ability to evaluate Kingdom opportunities and his ever present sense of humor were persuasive, created confidence and made it delightful to work with him.

The memories of my administrative activities and experiences as Executive Secretary among these Conferences, those with the Lexington Conference and such men as Dr. Skelton will always abide in appreciative recognition of their splendid and heroic achievements.

With cordial greetings, I am

Sincerely yours,
F. W. MUELLER

F. W. MUELLER

HISTORY OF THE LEXINGTON CONFERENCE

Illinois Wesleyan University
BLOOMINGTON, ILLINOIS
Merrill J. Holmes, Vice-President

March 2, 1946

Through frequent official visits to the Lexington Conference during three quadrenniums of service as Secretary for Education Institutions for Negroes of the Methodist Board of Education, I had some opportunity to observe the far-flung service of that Conference, which had done pioneer work in several North Central states. Its statesmanlike leaders include Dr. David E. Skelton, whose outstanding service in the expanding work of that Conference through many years well qualifies him to write its history.

M. J. HOLMES
Vice-President
Illinois Wesleyan University

HISTORY OF THE LEXINGTON CONFERENCE

Edwin Holt Hughes

691 ROLLINWOOD DRIVE
CHEVY CHASE, MARYLAND
Retired Bishop
The Methodist Church

Dear D. E.:

I enclose a short memograph for your history. I have held the session of the Lexington Conference twice—once at Dayton, once at Louisville. Both sessions had much responsibility but great joy.

In its membership I have had three close friends—David E. Skelton, Elam A. White and E. Wesley Kinchen. The last named went early home to God. He was a good true man and I have greatly mourned his absence from our circle of work.

I confidently assist in handing on the assets of the Conference to its present preachers and to its fine laymen, God bless them all!

Cordially,

EDWIN H. HUGHES

HISTORY OF THE LEXINGTON CONFERENCE
Central Jurisdiction of The Methodist Church

BALTIMORE AREA

ALEXANDER P. SHAW, RESIDENT BISHOP

1206 Etting Street

Baltimore 17, Md.

Rev. David E. Skelton   February 8, 1946
321 West 29th Street
Indianapolis, Indiana

Dear Brother Skelton:

    I am sending you a photograph of myself from which a cut may be made. I do not have a good picture of Mrs. Shaw. She does not like to be photographed.

    Hoping this will be sufficient, so that you may go ahead with your history, I am

                                Sincerely yours,

                                    A. P. SHAW

College of Bishops

CENTRAL JURISDICTION

BISHOP ROBERT E. JONES
Elected May, 1920
Des Moines, Iowa

BISHOP MATTHEW W. CLAIRE
Elected May, 1920
Des Moines, Iowa

HISTORY OF THE LEXINGTON CONFERENCE

BISHOP ALEXANDER P. SHAW
Elected May, 1936
Columbus, Ohio

BISHOP W. A. C. HUGHES
Elected June, 1940
St. Louis, Mo.

BISHOP L. H. KING
Elected June, 1940
St. Louis, Mo.

BISHOP W. J. KING
Elected June, 1944
Greensboro, N. C.

BISHOP R. N. BROOKS
Elected June, 1944
Greensboro, N. C.

BISHOP EDWIN W. KELLEY
Elected June, 1944
Greensboro, N. C.

HISTORY OF THE LEXINGTON CONFERENCE

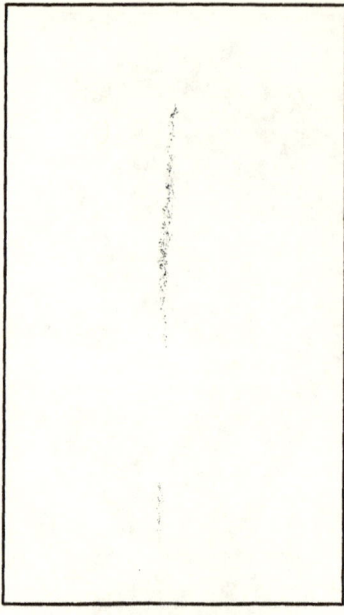

A. P. CAMPHOR
May, 1916
Saratoga, N. Y.

Bishop I. B. Scott, Missionary Bishop to Africa, 1904, Los Angeles, Cal., elected Bishop A. P. Camphor, May, 1916, Saratoga, N. Y.

Historical Sessions of the Conference

The Lexington Annual Conference of The Methodist Church was organized in March, 1869, and has held annual sessions as follows:

Yr.	Mo.	Place	Bishop	Secretary
1870	March	Louisville, Ky.	Edward Thompson	E. C. Moore
1971	March	Lexington, Ky.	Davis W. Clark	E. C. Moore
1872	March	Maysville, Ky.	Levi Scott	L. W. Jenkins
1873	March	Bowling Green, Ky.	Matthew Simpson	M. W. Taylor
1874	March	Cincinnati, Ohio	Stephen M. Marrill	M. W. Taylor
1875	March	Louisville, Ky.	Randolph S. Foster	M. W. Taylor
1876	March	Lexington, Ky.	Isaac W. Wiley	M. W. Taylor
1877	March	Maysville, Ky.	Thomas Bowman	M. W. Taylor
1878	March	Indianapolis, Ind.	Jesse T. Peck	E. W. S. Hamm
1879	March	Louisville, Ky.	Isaac W. Wiley	E. W. S. Hamm
1880	March	Paris, Ky.	Matthew Simpson	E. W. S. Hamm
1881	March	Springfield, Ohio	Isaac W. Wiley	E. W. S. Hamm
1882	March	Louisville, Ky.	Randolph S. Foster	Joseph Courtney
1883	March	Lexington, Ky.	Ed. G. Andrews	Joseph Courtney
1884	March	Covington, Ky.	Cyrus D. Foss	H. W. Tate
1885	April	Springfield, Ohio	Thomas Bowman	H. W. Tate
1886	April	Bowling Green, Ky.	William L. Harris	H. W. Tate
1887	April	Indianapolis, Ind.	W. F. Mallalieu	H. W. Tate
1888	April	Cincinnati, Ohio	Stephen M. Merrill	H. W. Tate
1889	March	Paris, Ky.	Ed. G. Andrews	H. W. Tate
1890	March	Louisville, Ky.	J. N. Fitzgerald	G. A. Sissle
1891	March	Lexington, Ky.	Isaac W. Joyce	E. L. Gilliam
1892	March	Indianapolis, Ind.	John M. Walden	E. L. Gilliam
1893	March	Shelbyville, Ky.	Randolph S. Foster	E. L. Gilliam
1894	March	Covington, Ky.	Daniel A. Goodsell	E. L. Gilliam
1895	March	Maysville, Ky.	John F. Hurst	E. A. White
1896	March	Louisville, Ky.	Thomas Bowman	E. A. White
1897	April	Springfield, Ohio	Cyrus D. Foss	E. A. White
1898	March	Terre Haute, Ind.	Charles H. Fowler	E. A. White
1899	March	Paris, Ky.	John H. Vencent	E. A. White
1900	March	Covington, Ky.	Stephens M. Merrill	E. A. White
1901	March	Indianapolis, Ind.	Stephen M. Merrill	E. A. White
1902	March	Mt. Zion, Cincinnati, Ohio	Daniel A. Goodsell	D. E. Skelton
1903	March	Chicago, Ill.	J. M. Walden	D. E. Skelton
1904	March	Lexington, Ky.	W. F. Mallalieu	J. W. Robinson
1905	March	Louisville, Ky.	J. W. Hamilton	J. W. Robinson
1906	March	Columbus, Ohio	H. W. Warren	J. W. Robinson
1907	March	Paris, Ky.	W. F. McDowell	J. W. Robinson
1908	March	Park, St. Cincinnati, Ohio	David H. Moore	J. W. Robinson
1909	March	Indianapolis, Ind.	W. F. Anderson	H. R. Wiley
1910	March	Maysville, Ky.	Earl Cranston	W. H. Riley
1911	March 29	Springfield, Ohio	E. H. Hughes	W. H. Riley
1912	March 27	11th St., Columbus, Ohio	Robert McIntyre	W. H. Riley
1913	March 26	Coke Chapel Louisville, Ky.	F. D. Leete	W. H. Riley
1914	March 18	Owensboro, Ky.	W. F. Anderson	W. H. Riley
1915	April 14	Fulton St. Chicago, Ill.	W. F. Anderson	W. H. Riley
1916	April 5	Jackson St. Louisville, Ky.	W. F. Anderson	W. H. Riley
1917	April 11	Park St. Cincinnati, Ohio	W. F. Anderson	W. H. Riley
1918	April 10	St. Mark's Chicago, Ill.	Thomas Nicholson	W. H. Riley
1919	April 9	Asbury, Lexington, Ky.	Thomas Nicholson	W. H. Riley
1920	April 7	Springfield, Ohio	W. F. Anderson	W. H. Riley
1921	April 20	Cory, Cleveland, Ohio	F. D. Leete	W. H. Riley
1922	April 19	Covington, Ky.	F. D. Leete	W. H. Riley
1923	April 11	Simpson, Indianapolis, Ind.	R. E. Jones	W. H. Riley
1924	April 9	Jones Temple, Louisville, Ky.	F. D. Leete	S. E. Grannum
1925	April 22	Dayton, Ohio	M. W. Clair	S. E. Grannum
1926	April 14	Mt. Zion, Cincinnati, Ohio	Theo S. Henderson	S. E. Grannum
1927	April 27	Simpson, Indianapolis, Ind.	C. E. Loske	S. E. Grannum
1928	April 11	South Park, Chicago, Ill.	M. W. Clair	S. E. Grannum
1929	April 11	Asbury, Lexington, Ky.	Edgar Blake	J. W. Chinn
1930	April 23	Scott, Detroit, Mich.	N. M. Clair	J. M. Chinn
1931	April 22	Jones Temple, Louisville, Ky.	E. H. Hughes	W. H. Wallace
1932	April 13	Calvary, Cincinnati, Ohio	M. W. Clair	W. H. Wallace
1933	April 26	Indiana Ave. Chicago, Ill.	M. W. Clair	W. H. Wallace
1934	April 19	Simpson, Indianapolis, Ind.	M. W. Clair	W. H. Wallace
1935	April 10	McKinley, Dayton, Ohio	H. Lester Smith	W. H. Wallace
1936	April 15	St. Mark's, Chicago, Ill.	M. W. Clair	W. H. Wallace

HISTORY OF THE LEXINGTON CONFERENCE

Yr.	Mo.		Place	Bishop	Secretary
1937	April	1	Asbury, Lexington, Ky.	R. E. Jones	S. P. Jenkins
1938	April	20	Cory, Cleveland, Ohio	A. P. Shaw	S. P. Jenkins
1939	April	12	Jones Temple, Louisville, Ky.	R. E. Jones	S. P. Jenkins
1940	April	12	Cincinnati, Ohio	R. E. Jones	S. P. Jenkins
1941	April	30	Centenary, Columbus, Ohio	R. E. Jones	S. P. Jenkins
1942	April	15	Detroit, Mich.	R. E. Jones	S. P. Jenkins
1943	May	9	Indianapolis, Ind.	R. E. Jones	S. P. Jenkins
1944	March	30	Cincinnati, Ohio	R. E. Jones	S. P. Jenkins
1945	April	18	Cincinnati, Ohio	E. W. Kelly	S. Marion Riley, Jr.
1946	April	24	Detroit, Mich.	E. W. Kelly	S. Marion Riley, Jr.
1947	April	9	Chicago, Ill.	E. W. Kelly	S. Marion Riley, Jr.
1948	April	4	Cleveland, Ohio	E. W. Kelly	S. Marion Riley, Jr.
1949	May	18	Indianapolis, Ind.	E. W. Kelly	S. Marion Riley, Jr.

Unsung Heroes

OF THE LEXINGTON CONFERENCE

Many of the men who never held an office in the Conference are the men who laid the foundation. Some of these men never received as much as $600 salary, yet were cheerful and happy, and now they speak to us from the beyond and are saying, "Carry on." The names listed below were church builders.

Andrew Bryant—1
George W. Downing—3
Crosby McPheeters—1
Elijah Henderson—1
Abraham Booker—2
J. W. Horton—1
Marcue McCoomer—2
Jessie Monday—1
Felix Ross—2
L. C. Harris—2
Thos. Tompkins—3
Green W. Powell—1
Joel Perkins—1
Zachariah Winchester—2
Wm. Braxton Daniels—2
W. C. Jenkins—1
J. H. L. Franklin—3
B. J. Coleman—1
Jno. F. Moreland—2
H. W. Tate—1
Hanson Tolbert—1
Wm. H. Burch—1
N. L. Carr—1
M. B. Lewis—1
Thos. M. Tompkins—1
Henry Gibson—1
Alex Posey—1
W. H. Lawrence—1
John Dowens—1
John W. Russell—1

D. E. Skelton—2; parsonage—1
C. J. Nichols—1
N. H. Tolbert—1
Chas. Pyles—1
S. G. Turner—3
W. H. Pope—1
Fred White—1
Trueman F. Williams—1
Chas. Ball—1
Jno. S. Bailey—1
W. A. Wells—1
A. Hargrove—1
Geo. W. Adams—1
Jno. W. Moreland, Sr.—2
Wm. Johnson—1
J. H. Hargrave—1
Alexander McDade—2
Creed H. Taylor—1
Adam Nunn—1
Logan Miles—1
Wm. H. Evans—3
Ezra D. Miller—1
Edward Lewis—1
J. A. Smith—1
Henry Steen—1
T. T. Carpenter—2
James Bowren—1
B. J. Strider—1
F. S. Delaney—1
Thos. L. Ferguson—1

Wm. H. Dickson—1

The figures indicate churches built or purchased, also parsonages purchased.

These are the men who followed up and paid church and parsonage debts and built up the membership:

C. C. Moore
Alex Adams
I. B. Hocker
J. G. Jones
H. A. Southgate
D. W. Heston
R. H. Willis
W. H. Heston
H. H. Hinton
N. A. Elliott
E. W. Kinchen

H. H. Good
Geo. W. Harris
J. H. Parker
F. W. Kenney
Randolph Pugh
W. H. Hopewell
A. A. Woolfolk
T. L. Wilson
Geo. W. Bailey
D. A. Oglesby
F. R. Robinson

HISTORY OF THE LEXINGTON CONFERENCE

S. H. Ferguson
W. T. Hayes
J. H. Love
A. R. Martin
S. S. Jessell
N. Sanders
Zale Ross
Jno. H. Jackson
C. T. Lewis

W. H. Vaughn
H. C. Buckner
W. H. Poindexter
H. C. Cooper
W. S. Harris
E. A. Driver
Geo. F. Carr
Geo. W. Staples
J. H. W. Pinkney

REV. GEORGE DOWNING

Rev. George Downing was one of the greatest evangelists the Lexington Conference ever produced. In one of his reports to the Conference he reported 484 conversions and 718 additions to the church in one year.

Other evangelists of the Conference were: T. M. Tompkins, Isaac Mason, Felix Ross, Henry White, W. W. Locke, W. H. Vaughn. James Bouren, Moses Lewis, W. H. Pope, Marcus McCoomer, J. L. Franklin, W. D. Patton, Richard Hughes, H. M. Carroll, C. E. Ball. These men were great in their field. George Downing stands at the head of the column—blessings to his memory.

OUR SUPPLY PASTORS

The early crusaders were: William Dickerson, William Baltimore, Isiah Mason, Thomas Brown, Frank Shipman, Aaron Broaddus, William Brown, Rev. Bean, Ben Bradley, Rev. Dr. Peters, M.D., Joel Bradshaw, Charlie Cottrell and B. W. Holloway.

P. S.—If your church history does not appear it is because your pastor at the time did not fill out and answer the questionnaire.

D. E. S.

DR. E. W. HAMMOND

Dr. E. W. S. Hammond was one of the great preachers of Methodism. He was proud of the Lexington Conference and ministers and laymen were very proud of him. He was three times Presiding Elder and District Superintendent. Served one term as editor of the Southwestern *Christian Advocate;* Dean of the Biblical Department of Walden University, Nashville, Tenn. His widow and daughter live in Cincinnati, his son resides in Indianapolis, Ind.

D. E. S.

Presiding Elders and District Superintendents
1869-1946

The Presiding Elders and District Superintendents of the Lexington Conference from 1869 to 1946.

LEXINGTON DISTRICT

Henry Lytle—4 years
D. P. Jones—2 years
Israel Simms—4 years
Daniel Jones—4 years
Henry W. White—4 years
John H. Stanley—6 years
Daniel Jones—9 months
Willis W. Locke—3 months
Joseph Courtney—6 years
Louis M. Hagood—5 years
John H. Stanley—6 years
P. T. Gorham—5 years
J. B. Redmond—6 years
H. M. Carrol—6 years
Samuel H. Sweeney—6 weeks
L. E. Jordon—4 years
F. R. Arnold—6 years
D. D. Turpeau, Sr.—5 years
W. H. Wallace—5 years

LOUISVILLE DISTRICT

Henderson Talbott—2 years
W. L. Muir—4 years
D. P. Jones—4 years
Monmouth Walton—4 years
M. W. Taylor—2 years
W. W. Locke—3 years
George W. Thomas—2 years
George A. Sissle—6 years
E. W. S. Hammond—4 years
Joseph Courtney—6 years
H. W. Tate—3 years
John W. Robinson—2 years
R. L. Dickerson—2 years
J. E. Wood—6 years
R. F. Broaddus—6 years
George W. Tindull—4 years
W. L. Noel—4 years
D. E. Skelton—5 years
Thomas H. Hines—6 years
D. M. Jordon—2 years

BOWLING GREEN DISTRICT
1873 to 1894—Discontinued in 1894

Henry Lytle—2 years
Zale Ross—4 years
Scott Ward—4 years
Abraham Booker—4 years
Daniel Jones—4 years
L. M. Hagood—3 years
T. L. Ferguson—1 year

INDIANA DISTRICT
1875 to 1922

W. L. Muir—2 years
W. C. Echols—4 years
E. W. S. Hammond—4 years
Charles Jones—4 years
W. S. Rollins—5 years
E. L. Gilliam—6 years
George A. Sissle—6 years
D. E. Skelton—6 years
G. R. Bryant—5 years
Joseph Courtney—2 years
E. A. White—3 years

CHICAGO-INDIANA DISTRICT

D. E. Skelton—1 year
P. T. Gorham—6 years
W. T. Davis—2 years
B. F. Smith—8 years
W. H. Williams—3 years
H. M. Carroll—4 years

HISTORY OF THE LEXINGTON CONFERENCE

COLUMBUS DISTRICT
1873 to 1946

W. C. Echols—4 years
W. L. Muir—2 years
M. W. Taylor—4 years
E. W. S. Hammond—3 years
M. S. Johnson—5 years
T. L. Ferguson—6 years
H. W. Simmons—2 years
E. A. White—6 years
Joseph Courtney—6 years

D. E. Skelton—5 years
T. L. Ferguson—6 years
S. H. Sweeney—2 years
E. A. White—4 years
John W. Robinson—2 years
J. H. Stennett—2 years
P. T. Gorham—4 years
W. H. Williams—3 years
W. H. McCallum—6 years

MAYSVILLE DISTRICT
1901 to 1924

E. A. White—4 years
George W. Zeigler—4 years

John S. Bailey—6 years
H. A. Foreman—6 years

INDIANA DISTRICT—Re-established
1938 to 1946

D. E. Skelton—2 years

John W. Patton—6 years

PRESENT CABINET

Chicago District, H. M. Carroll—4 year
Cincinnati District, Alfred Clay—3 years
Columbus District, S. P. Jenkins—3 years

Indiana District, H. O. McCutchin—2 years
Louisville District, H. H. Green—2 years.

CABINET MEMBERS FOR 1950

These brethren compose the Cabinet of 1950 who will assist Bishop E. W. Kelly in the assignments of the pastors for 1950.

Chicago District: H. M. Carroll, B.D., D.D., District Superintendent. Closing his fourth year. Rev. Carroll is the little giant of the Conference. He has been faithful and worked hard.

Cincinnati Lexington District: Alford Clay, District Superintendent. Closing his fifth year. Rev. Clay is a great preacher and has shown marked leadership. His future is very promising.

Columbus District: S. P. Jenkins, District Superintendent. Closing his third year. Rev. Jenkins is very positive, yet kind. He wants things done and gets results. He has a bright future.

Indiana District: H. O. McCutchin, District Superintendent. Rev. McCutchin is closing his third year with wonderful success. He has brought the district forward in a fine way. His successor will find a well organized district and a fine group of pastors. May his future continue bright.

Louisville District: H. H. Green, District Superintendent. Closing his second year and is showing great leadership. He believes in the

Scripture where in St. Paul it says, "Show me your faith without works and I will show you my faith by my works." Rev. Green knows his district from A to Z. We predict great things under the able leadership of this young man.

Chronological Roll
LEXINGTON ANNUAL CONFERENCE

No.	Name	Year	No.	Name	Year
1.	D. E. Skelton	1891	56.	G. W. Hall	1926
2.	J. E. Wood	1892	57.	W. O. Calvest	1927
3.	W. L. Darius	1897	58.	J. H. Grinnage	1927
5.	William McMorries	1899	59.	B. F. Holloway	1927
6.	P. T. Gorham	1900	60.	S. P. Jenkins	1927
7.	W. A. Hinton	1900	61.	C. M. Sexton	1927
8.	D. D. Turpeau, Sr.	1902	62.	S. T. Jones	1927
9.	J. M. Harris	1903	63.	D. J. Price	1927
10.	H. M. Carroll	1907	64.	F. C. Walker	1927
11.	G. W. Tindull	1907	65.	Alfred Clay	1927
12.	H. B. Mays	1911	66.	I. R. Sumner	1928
13.	B. F. Smith	1912	67.	S. W. Bankhead	1928
14.	B. H. Williams	1912	68.	L. R. Simmons	1928
15.	J. S. Roberts	1912	69.	J. H. Simpson	1928
17.	J. D. Rice	1912	70.	C. H. Wilkins	1928
18.	J. H. Ellis	1912	71.	C. M. Harris	1929
19.	E. E. Crawford	1916	72.	W. D. Patton	1929
20.	W. E. White	1917	73.	S. M. Riley, Jr.	1929
21.	J. W. Chinn	1918	74.	C. T. R. Nelson	1930
22.	O. H. Banks	1918	76.	Damon P. Young	1930
23.	W. P. Kellogg	1918	77.	E. L. Briggs	1931
24.	C. T. Parker	1918	78.	W. H. McCallum	1931
25.	J. W. Crook	1919	79.	H. H. Green	1932
26.	Richard Hughes	1919	80.	M. L. Harris	1932
27.	I. C. Smith	1919	81.	P. H. E. Winfield	1933
28.	F. R. Arnold	1920	82.	C. V. Haynes	1934
29.	G. G. Morgan	1920	83.	Thomas Hines	1935
30.	W. H. Wallace	1920	84.	Squire B. Lester	1935
31.	William II. W. Williams	1920	85.	E. Dougan	1935
32.	M. W. Clair, Jr.	1920	86.	Alvin Burton	1936
33.	J. C. Hayes	1921	87.	Arthur Davis	1936
34.	S. E. Grannum	1921	88.	B. F. Shockley	1936
35.	C. J. Johnson	1921	89.	Hermes Zimmerman	1936
36.	C. L. Fleming	1922	90.	William A. Greene	1936
37.	M. L. Bellinger	1922	91.	C. D. Stemley	1936
38.	H. M. Marbly	1922	92.	J. I. Dixon	1936
39.	B. F. Neal	1912	93.	I. D. Dorsey	1936
40.	C. H. Brower	1932	94.	J. F. Hewitt	1938
41.	R. E. Skelton	1922	95.	A. D. Williams	1939
42.	D. M. Jordan	1923	96.	A. R. Howard, Jr.	1939
43.	G. W. Sherard	1923	97.	Merrill E. Nelson	1940
44.	H. O. McCutchin	1923	98.	V. D. Elliott	1940
45.	O. B. Quick	1924	99.	Norman J. Long	1940
46.	H. E. Chapman	1924	100.	F. F. McCallum	1939
47.	R. G. Morris	1917	101.	Junius D. Hall	1943
48.	E. E. Hamblen	1924	102.	Thomas L. Tinsley	1943
49.	C. C. Miller	1924	103.	Paul L. Ayer	1944
50.	Robert Braxton	1924	104.	Paul V. Smith	1944
51.	J. W. Patton	1925	105.	Melvin F. Hardin	1944
52.	J. P. Pierce	1925	106.	R. M. Robison	1944
53.	L. R. Stark	1925	107.	Samuel Ross Wright	1944
55.	W. L. Giles	1926	108.	Maceo Pembroke	1945

The First Race Man to Hold Our Conference

DR. JOS. COURTNEY
Louisville, Ky., March 26, 1913

The Lexington Conference met in New Coke Methodist Episcopal Church. Devotionals conducted by Charles Jones. The following telegrams were read:

Chicago, Illinois. REV. D. E. SKELTON, Lexington Conference, Louisville, Ky.
Proceed with the election of president. Impossible to reach the Conference. Elect a president.
WM. F. McDOWELL

R. L. Dickerson: "I move the election of Dr. Joseph Courtney."
E. L. Gilliam: "I second the motion."
He was elected and presided each day until April 2, 1913.

Chicago, Illinois. D. E. SKELTON:
Contact Bishop Leete. Have him come for the ordination.
WM. F. McDOWELL

This committee was appointed to contact Bishop Leete: Dr. L. M. Hagood, D. E. Skelton, J. S. Bailey.

April 1, 1913. REV. D. E. SKELTON:
Will arrive Wednesday, April 2, 1913.
F. D. LEETE

9:30 A.M., April 2, 1913, Bishop F. D. Leete arrived and assumed the presidency of the Conference.

After the ordination of W. H. Redmon, Deacon; James S. Boling and Elijah A. Driver as Elders, Bishop Leete made the following remarks to the Conference:

"Brethren: I have just met with the Cabinet. The District Superintendents have done their work so thoroughly under the guidince of Dr. Courtney, your president, that I could not improve on what has been done. You have a fine Cabinet and a great leader in Dr. Courtney."

The Church Women's Work

THE LADIES AID SOCIETY

The Society was organized by Mrs. Minerva Harvey, sister to Rev. Dr. E. L. Gilliam, in 1914, and the work of the Aid Society under her leadership was outstanding.

Mrs. Harvey never tired in her work, and the ministers often spoke of her as the Angel of Mercy and Help in the Annual and District Conferences.

She urged the women to work harder, to help the church in its finances in the local church and our general benevolence. Every Aid Society in the Conference received a letter from Sister Harvey during the year and the chief topic was WORK.

The Woman's Foreign Missionary Society was organized by Mrs. J. T. Leggett.

HISTORY OF THE MINISTERS' WIVES ASSOCIATION OF THE LEXINGTON CONFERENCE

At Asbury Church, Lexington, April 11, 1919, Mrs. Anna Stanley Foreman suggested that the ministers' wives of the Lexington Conference organize into a group that we might know each other better and love each other more.

We organized and Mrs. Pezavia O'Connell was elected our first President and Mrs. Helen Penn was elected Secretary.

The By-Laws were drawn up by Mrs. J. L. Franklin, Mrs. R. L. Dickerson and Mrs. J. H. Ross.

Our next President was Mrs. John Robinson with Mrs. Helen Penn, Secretary. In April, 1924, Mrs. R. F. Broaddus was elected President, Mrs. Helen Penn, Secretary.

In 1925, Mrs. R. F. Broaddus was re-elected President, Mrs. W. P. Kellogg was elected Secretary.

At this meeting we agreed to bring a substantial sum the next year to be given to the Board of Pensions and Relief. Ten dollars was to be raised by each minister's wife aside from the fifty cents yearly dues which we distributed at our annual meeting.

We were very successful and turned over to the Board, $622.25. Thus our permanent fund was established.

From 1925 to 1929 Mrs. Broaddus and Mrs. Kellogg were President and Secretary respectively. During this period $1,925.47 was raised for Pensions and Relief. In 1929 Mrs. F. R. Arnold was elected President and Mrs. E. A. White, Secretary. In 1932 Mrs. F. R. Arnold was elected President and Mrs. J. W. Patton, Secretary.

HISTORY OF THE LEXINGTON CONFERENCE

MRS. W. H. WALLACE

In 1934 Mrs. Arnold was re-elected President and Mrs. W. P. Kellogg, Secretary. In 1941 Mrs. J. W. Patton was elected President; Mrs. W. P. Kellogg, Secretary. In 1944 Mrs. O. B. Quick was elected President; Mrs. W. P. Kellogg, Secretary. In 1945 Mrs. J. S. Roberts was elected President; Mrs. W. P. Kellogg, Secretary.

Our Treasurers during this period were: Mrs. J. E. Wood and Mrs. T. L. Ferguson, each serving several years and our present Treasurer, Mrs. W. H. Wallace, who has been serving for several years.

Monies put into Board of Pensions and Relief to April, 1944, $6,183.81.

Besides this, our annual dues of fifty cents have been collected and disbursed at the Annual Conference meetings to them that might be able to use it.

The Permanent Fund has $10,084.23. Given to members' wives, $1,160.00.

President, 1949, Mrs. J. I. Dixon.

THE WOMEN'S WORK IN THE CONFERENCE

The Woman's Home Missionary Society was organized in the Ninth Street Church, Covington, Ky., on March 23, 1900, and continued for forty years. Mrs. James Dale (white), President of the Ohio Conference, presided during the organization and election.

42

HISTORY OF THE LEXINGTON CONFERENCE

The first Lexington Conference officers were: President, Mrs. J. T. Leggett; Vice-President, Rev. Mrs. Dollie Lewis; Corresponding Secretary, Mrs. Erma Harris; Recording Secretary, Miss Ella B. Brown; Treasurer, Mrs. Rush Corburn; Managers, Mrs. A. B. West, Mrs. Mary E. Scarce, Mrs. Garner, Mrs. D. E. Skelton. Others in attendance: Mrs. Mattie Sissle, Mrs. D. R. Hickman, Mrs. Martha Campbell, Mrs. Martha Waldon, Mrs. Geo. W. Ziegler, Rev. J. T. Leggett, and Rev. D. E. Skelton.

Each of these paid $1.20 yearly dues and the organization became the W.H.M.S. of the Lexington Conference. From this meeting the women went forth and began the organization of district and local societies, and within three years all the districts were organized and reported from twelve to eighteen societies. The Conference reached its zenith in membership and money during the forty years. In 1922.

From 1922 to 1940 the following women served as Presidents: Mrs. J. T. Leggett, Mrs. Mattie Sissle, Mrs. Anna Stanley Foreman, Mrs. Jessie T. Scott, and Mrs. A. D. Turpeau, Sr.

HISTORY OF THE LEXINGTON CONFERENCE

WOMAN'S SOCIETY OF CHRISTIAN SERVICE
ST. LOUIS AREA—CENTRAL JURISDICTION

MRS. ADDYE W. WARE

We present to you the first President of the Woman's Society of Christian Service, Mrs. Addye W. Ware, and her co-workers in the Lexington Conference: Mrs. Fannie L. Kellogg, Mrs. W. H. Wallace, Mrs. Oberia Patton, Mrs. G. W. Sherard, Mrs. Lethia M. King, Mrs. Georgia H. Gamlett and Mrs. L. M. Yancy.

No woman in the Conference ever had such a difficult task as Mrs. Ware did in welding together the W.H.M.S., the Ladies Aid Society, and the W.F.M.S. But during the quadrennium she was able to turn over to her successor a complete organization of the Conference, the largest group of women ever known in one organization.

Mrs. Ware will be remembered with gratitude for her excellent leadership, her timely advice, her kind affectionate and loving spirit in guiding the women through the transition. What more can we say than, "Heaven's benediction be yours in the many years to come."

The present President, Mrs. W. H. Wallace—welcome to you. You have before you a taxing task, but a wonderful opportunity. The women who elected you believed in you and there is no doubt in their minds as to your leadership, ability and Christian spirit. You will lead the W.S.C.S. to wonderful achievement—the slogan, GO FORWARD!

HISTORY OF THE LEXINGTON CONFERENCE

1949. To Mrs. Lucile Wilkins, those who have preceded you leave behind their record, take hold and go forward. Blessings be yours.
D. E. S.

LIST OF OFFICERS
Addye W. Ware ....President
Mrs. D. M. Jordan ....Vice-President
Mrs. W. P. Kellogg ....Recording Secretary
Mrs. W. H. Wallace ....Corresponding Secretary
Mrs. J. W. Patton ....Treasurer
Mrs. Letha Mae King ....Secretary of Wesleyan Service Guild
Mrs. D. D. Turpeau, Mrs. S. B. Lester ....Secretary of Student Work
Mrs. Frannie B. May Dorsey ....Secretary of Children's Work
Mrs. Lucille Wilkins, Mrs. Kathleen Bright
  Secretary of Young Women and Girls
Mrs. S. P. Jenkins.........Secretary of Missionary Education and Service
Mrs. G. W. Sherard
  Secretary of Christian Social Relations and Local Church Activities
Mrs. L. V. Yancey, Mrs. Cassia A. Morris
  Secretary of Literature and Publications
Mrs. Clara F. Webster ....Secretary of Supplies
Mrs. Georgia C. Hamlett ....Secretary of Spiritual Life
Mrs. Emily Rutherford, Mrs. R. Lucille Porter. Secretary of Status of Women
Mrs. Ethel Clair ....Secretary of Missionary Personal

DISTRICT PRESIDENTS
Chicago—Mrs. Mildred Watkins, Mrs. Louise Cooper.
Cincinnati—Mrs. Damon P. Young, Mrs. Lucy Harth Smith.
Columbus—Mrs. Annie Mae Porter, Mrs. Myra Carter, Miss Elizabeth Langford.
Indianapolis—Mrs. Lulu G. Bean.
Louisville—Mrs. Clara F. Webster, Miss Lilly M. Miller.
Mrs. W. H. Wallace from 1944 to 1948.
Mrs. Lucile Wilkins from 1948 to 1952.

LOUISVILLE-EVANSVILLE DISTRICT
321 West 29th St.
Indianapolis, Ind.
January, 1937

My dear Sister:

The Director of the Women's Department of the Million Unit Fellowship Movement, Mrs. J. M. Avann, has appointed me to head up this movement on the Evansville-Louisville District.

May I request that you organize your church womanhood and have a tea to be known as the International Fellowship Tea, at which time you will take a silver offering to be sent to me. I will forward what you send to Mrs. Bishop Robert E. Jones. This movement is intended to stimulate a greater interest in the Million Unit Fellowship. I am asking your women to raise $——— and send to me by March 1, 1937. I will send the reports to Mrs. Jones. Your church will receive World's Service Voucher.

As women let us do our part. With very best wishes. I am
Sincerely yours,
GEORGIA M. SKELTON

S:R

Through this appeal the district met its quota.

Laymen's Work

DR. DENNIS A. BETHEA

I am presenting the photo of Dr. Dennis A. Bethea, of Hammond, Ind. He was born in Dillon, S. C., October 16, ——, and received his college preparatory work at Princess Ann Academy (now Princess Ann Junior College) in Maryland. He did his college work at Allegheny College, Meadville, Pa., and took his medical degree from the Chicago Medical School in 1907. After a few years practice in Terre Haute, Ind., he entered the Harvard Medical School in Boston for postgraduate work.

Dr. Bethea is a member of the American and the National Medical Associations, and is on the staff of St. Margaret Hospital in Hammond, which is one of the largest in the state. He has done considerable writing for newspapers and magazines. For many years he conducted health columns in the Southwestern *Christian Advocate* and the *Christian Recorder*. At present he is the health editor on the Afro American Newspapers of Baltimore and Washington.

Dennis Bethea has always taken a lively interest in church affairs. During his college days in Chicago he was a Sunday school teacher and chief usher in the St. Mark Church. He has been a member of four General Conferences including the Uniting Conference. For thirty years he was at the head of the Laymen Association of the

Lexington Conference. He is trustee and lay leader in the Delaney Methodist Church in Gary, Ind.

Dr. Bethea's first marriage was to Miss Alice B. McLeod, daughter of the Rev. Jerry McLeod of the South Carolina Conference, and sister to Dr. E. C. McLeod, President of Wiley College. To this union there was born Mrs. Willa Tuttle of Carthage, Ind. His second marriage was to Miss Margaret Broadus of Jeffersonville, Ind., in 1925. To this union was born Norma Mae, who is fifteen and a sophomore in the Hammond High School.

B. F. SMITH

JOHN CURRENT

MRS. E. E. HAMBLIN

Mrs. E. E. Hamblin, wife of Rev. Hamblin, daughter of Dr. and Mrs. C. D. C. Mebane.

Mrs. Hamblin is a graduate of Clark University, Atlanta, Ga. Her father and mother each represented our Conference in the General Conference and should the church send Mrs. Hamblin she would reflect credit upon the Conference.

Mrs. Hamblin is a faithful worker in the W.S.C.S.

HISTORY OF THE LEXINGTON CONFERENCE

CHURCH SCHOOL SUPERINTENDENTS WHO HAVE SERVED TEN YEARS OR MORE

1. Chicago, Ill.—R. A. Crolley—40 years
2. Hawesville, Ky.—Stephen Miller—30 years
3. Flemingsburg, Ky.—David C. Shaw—27 years
4. Evansville, Ind.—Jeremiah Spotsville—22 years
5. Springfield, Ohio—Eliza Langford—20 years
6. Cleveland, Ohio (Cora)—Richard Sissle—17 years
7. Watson, Ind.—Brother Collier—16 years
8. Terre Haute, Ind.—John Montgomery—12 years
9. Louisville, Ky. (Jones)—Mrs. Jessie Scott—12 years
10. Princeton, Ind.—Mr. Lewis—12 years
11. Cincinnati, Ohio (Park St.)—Van Clinton—12 years
12. New Castle, Ind. Floyd Winslow—11 years
13. Rushville, Ind.—Nathan Fletcher—11 years
14. Chicago, Ill. (Fulton St.)—Dr. J. Frank Armstrong, M.D.—10 years
15. Cincinnati, Ohio—Ollie Fountaine—14 years
16. Indianapolis, Ind.—Amos Bibee—19 years
17. Indianapolis, Ind.—W. H. Blair—11 years
18. Indianapolis, Ind.—Wm. R. Hill—13 years.

JOHN A. WASHINGTON

Our St. Mark Church was organized in his home. Six members. Now has over 4,000 members. He also organized Fulton Street, now Gammon Memorial, then St. Matthew Church and Sunday school, also at 37th and Cottage Grove, now Hartzell Center. Racine, now St. Paul, Harvery and last furnished the music with his chorus at Indiana and 56th Street—peace to his memory.

HISTORY OF THE LEXINGTON CONFERENCE

J. C. TRAYLOR

I must associate with Brother Traylor, Rev. Walker and Rev. H. B. Mays. These three men believed that we should become a power in Detroit, and today we have five buildings and seven congregations, due to the untiring efforts of these men in their determination to establish Methodism in Detroit. Well done brethren, you deserve a reward.

JOHN A. PATTON

John A. Patton, one of Simpson's worthy laymen, son of a minister, one of the largest contributors of our Conference. Mr. Patton is a very successful undertaker, has a beautiful home in Indianapolis and a summer home in Idlewild, Mich. He reared two boys who will make their mark in life. The only place John A. Patton fails is on the lake in Idlewild—here his good wife teaches him how to fish.

HISTORY OF THE LEXINGTON CONFERENCE

Other laymen who should be mentioned: Richard A. Sissle, Prof. Spotiswood, Atty. J. Earnest Wilkins, B. Higgins, W. R. Hill, Dr. C. D. C. Mebane, J. H. Schooler, W. Jones, Mrs. Jesse Scott, Charley Hamilton, Dr. Emerson, Arby Owens, Martin Dean and many others space will not allow to all the good laymen of the Lexington Conference. May I say, "You have given us a great Conference."

OUR SUPPLY PASTORS

The early crusaders were: William Dickerson, William Baltimore, Isaiah Mason, Thomas Brown, Frank Shipman, Aaron Broaddus, William Brown, Rev. Bean, Ben Bradley, Rev. Peters, M.D., Joel Bradshaw, Charlie Cottrell and B. W. Holloway.

P. S. If your church history does not appear it is because your pastor at the time did not fill out and answer the questionnaire.

D. E. S.

The laymen of the Lexington Conference was organized in 1919. The first President was Dr. D. A. Bethea who served for thirty years. They have had only two Presidents—Dr. Bethea and Attorney J. Earnest Wilkins, who is now serving his eighth year.

The laymen of the Lexington Conference are very much interested in the advancement of the Conference. Since the organization of the Laymen's Association, the membership has increased 30 per cent. The benevolence 45 per cent, which shows what can be done with a live wide-awake Board of Laymen with great leadership like unto Dr. Bethea and Attorney Wilkins.

P. S. John A. Current, elected in 1948, is beginning his work in a fine way.

Statistical Review

CHICAGO DISTRICT
Loss, 1900 to 1946

	Property Value	Membership	Property Value	Membership
Racine	......	....	....	45
Wentworth Avenue	......	....	....	60
		Transferred to Minneapolis Conference		
Minneapolis	$ 3,000	....	Our Conference	80
	$ 3,000			185

CHICAGO
Gain, 1900 to 1946

	Property Value	Membership	Property Value	Membership
St. Mark	$ 2,000	315	$ 50,000	4,559
Gammon Memorial	......	....	30,000	557
Hartzell Memorial	......	....	50,000	1,567
Indiana Avenue	......	....	75,000	698
St. Matthew	......	....	....	435
Miller Street	......	....	....	132
	$ 2,000	315	$205,000	7,948

DETROIT DISTRICT

	Property Value	Membership	Property Value	Membership
Berea	......	....	$ 40,000	346
St. Paul	......	....	6,000	40
Second Grace	......	....	4,500	115
Mitchell Memorial	......	....	600	31
Scott	......	....	99,400	1,988
East Side	......	....	50,000	271
Evanston (Illinois)	......	....	4,000	36
Flint (Michigan)	......	....	4,000	55
Gary	......	....	75,000	582
Harvey	......	....	8,000	30
Pontiac (Michigan)	......	....	12,500	184
St. Paul (Minnesota)	......	....	27,000	238
St. Paul (Chicago)	......	....	11,000	67
			$340,000	3,951

CINCINNATI, LEXINGTON DISTRICT
Loss, 1900 to 1946

	Property Value	Membership	Property Value	Membership
Westwood	$ 1,500	36	....	....
Boyd (Kentucky)	500	40	....	....
Laries (Kentucky)	360	22	....	....
Milford (Kentucky)	......	22	....	....
New Providence (Kentucky)	300	40	....	....

HISTORY OF THE LEXINGTON CONFERENCE

	Property Value	Membership	Property Value	Membership
Corinth (Kentucky)	200	25	....	....
Poplar Plains (Kentucky)	200	22	....	....
Tilton (Kentucky)	150	30	....	....
Tolesboro (Kentucky)	300	30	....	....
Mt. Carmel (Kentucky)	400	30	....	....
Pleasantville	150	16	....	....
	$ 4,016	313		

GAIN, 1900 TO 1946

	Property Value	Membership	Property Value	Membership
Calvary	$ 9,000	126	$175,000	1,517
Mt. Zion	6,000	212	120,000	580
Cleves	......	....	600	31
Winchester	600	120	9,000	185
	$15,600	458	$304,600	2,313

COLUMBUS DISTRICT
Loss, 1900 TO 1946

	Property Value	Membership	Property Value	Membership
Bellaire	$ 700	40	....	....
Bridgeport	600	30	....	....
Flushing	300	17	....	....
Laurel	600	45	....	....
Georgetown	400	20	....	....
Mt. Healthy (Ohio)	500	40	....	....
22nd and Scoville (Cleveland)	......	125	....	....
Zanesville	......	60	....	....
	$ 3,100	365		

GAIN, 1900 TO 1946

	Property Value	Membership	Property Value	Membership
Akron	......	....	$ 18,000	300
Canton	......	....	3,000	90
Cleveland—Mt. Pleasant	......	....	20,000	225
Cleveland—Miles Heights	......	....	1,800	77
Columbus—Clair Chapel	......	....	3,000	61
Columbus—White Chapel	......	....	1,000	30
Springfield—Broaddus	......	....	1,180	118
Toledo	......	....	10,000	200
Youngstown	......	....	36,000	600
			$ 93,980	1,791

INDIANA DISTRICT
Loss, 1900 TO 1946

	Property Value	Membership	Property Value	Membership
Browns	$ 300	26	....	....
Cannelton	300	22	....	....
Cementville	200	40	....	....
Bloomington	700	46	....	....
Graville (Illinois)	300	26	....	....
Greencastle	300	27	....	....
Greenfield	700	27	....	....
Tell City	300	30	....	....

HISTORY OF THE LEXINGTON CONFERENCE

	Property Value	Membership	Property Value	Membership
Newburg	700	35	....	....
N. Terre Haute	250	26	....	....
Lawrence (Illinois)	200	24	....	....
	$ 4,250	329		

GAIN, 1900 TO 1946

	Property Value	Membership	Property Value	Membership
Scott—Indianapolis	......	....	$ 14,000	235
Munice	......	....	2,400	108
St. Paul—Indianapolis	......	....	1,000	35
New Albany	......	....	1,500	24
			$ 18,900	402

LOUISVILLE, BOWLING GREEN DISTRICT
Loss, 1900 TO 1946

	Property Value	Membership	Property Value	Membership
Osbourn	$ 300	22	....	....
Cedar Grove	......	15	....	....
Bedford	300	25	....	....
Boston	200	12	....	....
Glasgow	2,000	85	....	....
Drakesburg	800	18	....	....
Mt. Washington	300	20	....	....
Jericho	200	25	....	....
New Haven	200	10	....	....
Sulphur	300	18	....	....
Smithfield	300	26	....	....
Owington	1,200	45	....	....
Senora	600	27	....	....
Taylor Mines	200	31	....	....
	$ 6,900	399		

GAIN, 1900 TO 1946

	Property Value	Membership	Property Value	Membership
Louisville—Calvary	$ 300	65	$ 4,000	175
New Coke	1,100	112	8,000	365
Jones	4,000	312	45,000	476
Parkland	......	....	2,000	35
	$ 5,400	489	$ 59,000	1,051

Rushville, Indiana
November 9, 1945

Dr. D. E. Skelton

Dear Brother:

Please do not be angry at my delay. I didn't get your blank until last Saturday. I was sure I could fill the blank by finding an old Yearbook. I have looked and can't find one. This is as far as I can remember.

1. City, Beloit, Wisconsin.
2. Name, Beloit Methodist Episcopal.

HISTORY OF THE LEXINGTON CONFERENCE

3. About 1917 or 1918 by J. W. Golden.
4. About 50 or 60 members.
5. Presiding Elder, Dr. Bryant.
6. Pastor, J. H. Bunton.
Best wishes to you and your family.

(Signed) SARAH E. BUNTON

QUESTIONNAIRE
RUSHVILLE, INDIANA

City or Town—Rushville, Indiana.
Name of Church—Wesley Methodist.
When Organized—1874.
First Pastor—Lowry S. Straws.
First W.S.C.S. President—Bertha Burton.
Presiding Elder—W. L. Muir.
Present Pastor—John Wesley Chinn.
Number of Minister's Children—One.
Names of Minister's Children—Gladys Chinn Sampson.

CHICAGO, ILLINOIS

City or Town—Chicago 37, Illinois.
Name of Church—Indiana Avenue Methodist.
When Organized—October 21, 1928.
Number of Members—Seventeen.
First Pastor—Rev. Robert S. Mosby.
First Aid President—Mrs. Lelia Shirley.
First W.H.M.S. President—Mrs. Mary Ward.
First W.F.M.S. President—Mrs. Gertrude Day.
First W.S.C.S. President—Mrs. Annie S. Potter.
First Sunday School Superintendent—Rev. W. H. McCallum.
Number of Years He Served—One.
First Church Superintendent—W. A. Combs.
Number of Years He Served—Five.
Presiding Elder—Rev. P. T. Gorham.
Number of Years He Served—One.
Present Pastor—Rev. S. Marion Riley, Jr.
Number of Years He Served—Recently appointed.
Number of Minister's Children—One.
Names of Minister's Children—Phyllis Maxine Riley.

DETROIT, MICHIGAN

City or Town—Detroit 21, Michigan.
Name of Church—St. Paul Methodist.
When Organized—1924.
Number of Members—Six.
First Pastor—Rev. Charles Wilkins.
First Aid President—Mrs. C. D. Mitchell (deceased).
First W.H.M.S. President—Mrs. Minnie Wills (deceased).
First W.F.M.S. President—Mrs. C. White (deceased).
First W.S.C.S. President—Mrs. R. Hawkins.
First Sunday School Superintendent—Charles D. Mitchell (deceased).
Number of Years He Served—Three.
First Church School Superintendent—Mr. A. H. Lee (deceased).
Number of Years He Served—Four.
Presiding Elder—Rev. P. T. Gorham.

HISTORY OF THE LEXINGTON CONFERENCE

Number of Years He Served—Four.
Present Pastor—C. A. Trammell.
Number of Years He Served—Three.

NEW CASTLE, INDIANA

City or Town—New Castle, Indiana.
Name of Church—Wiley Methodist.
When Organized—1877.
Number of Members—Fourteen.
First Pastor—Rev. Daniel Tucker.
First Aid President—Mrs. W. W. Heston.
First W.H.M.S. President—Mrs. Ella Hill.
First W.F.M.S. President—Mrs. Cora Thurman.
First W.S.C.S. President—Mrs. Dollie Wright.
First Sunday School Superintendent—Rev. Sanford Holcomb.
Number of Years He Served—For a number of years.
First Church School Superintendent—Floyd Winslow.
Number of Years He Served—Eleven.
Presiding Elder—Rev. Hammond.
Number of Years He Served—Four.
Present Pastor—I. D. Dorsey.

TERRE HAUTE, INDIANA

Saulters Methodist Church. Organized, October, 1879.
Rev. Elie Lane—Pastor.
E. W. S. Hammond—Presiding Elder.
First Sunday School Superintendent—Albert Saulter.
First Aid President—Mrs. Sarah Wilson.
First W.H.M.S. President—Mrs. Rachel Statesman.
Mr. John Montgomery for Sunday School or Church School Superintendent for twelve years.
Mrs. Northy Taylor, Mrs. Mary Turner, Mrs. Dora Robbins, William Robbins, Sherman Purcell, P. J. Orr have served for twenty-two years as officers.

CHICAGO, ILLINOIS

Indiana Avenue Methodist Church. Organized, October 21, 1928.
First Pastor—Robert S. Mosby.
First Sunday School Superintendent—W. H. McCallum.
First Aid President—Mrs. Lelia Shirley.
First W.H.M.S. President—Mrs. Mary Ward.
First W.F.M.S. President—Mrs. Gertrude Day.
First W.S.C.S. President—Mrs. Annie Potter.
First District Superintendent—Dr. P. T. Gorham.
Longest term Church School Superintendent—W. A. Combs.

Saint Mark Methodist Church. Organized in 1891 by Dr. E. L. Gilliam.
Number of Members—Eight.
First Pastor—Rev. S. C. Goosley.
First Aid President—Mrs. Nellie Bomar.
First W.H.M.S. President—Mrs. R. A. Crolley.
First W.F.M.S. President—Mrs. Elizabeth Jackson.
First W.S.C.S. President—Lucile Wilkins.
First Sunday and Church School Superintendent—Mr. R. A. Crolley, served for thirty-five years.

RUSHVILLE, INDIANA

Wesley Methodist Church. Organized, 1874.
First Pastor—Lowrey S. Straws.
First W.S.C.S. President—Mrs. Bertha Burton.

HISTORY OF THE LEXINGTON CONFERENCE

First Presiding Elder—W. L. Muir.
Brother Nathan P. Fletcher served as Sunday School Superintendent for eleven years.

BELLOIT, WISCONSIN

Belloit Methodist Church. Orgainzed in 1917 by Rev. J. W. Golden.
Number of Members—Fifty.
Presiding Elder—Dr. G. R. Bryant.
This church has made a wonderful progress. The new church is worth $20,000 and has a membership of ninety-two.

PRINCETON, INDIANA

Calvary Methodist Church. Organized, 1880.
Number of Members—Six.
First Pastor—Rev. Mason.
First Aid President—Mrs. Adams.
First W.S.C.S. President—Mrs. Mary Lou Lyles.
Mr. Lewis served as Superintendent of Sunday School and Church School for twelve years.

EVANSVILLE, INDIANA

St. John Methodist Church.
First Pastor—Rev. Jessie Munday.
First Aid President—Mary Winfrey.
First W.H.M.S. President—Mrs. Annie Bell.
First W.F.M.S. President—Mrs. Sophronia Lambert.
First Superintendent of Sunday School—Wesley Irvin.
First Church School Superintendent—Jerimiah Spottsville, served twenty-one years.
First Presiding Elder—E. L. Gilliam.
Members Today—One hundred forty.
Church School Scholars—One hundred forty-five.

NEW CASTLE, INDIANA

Wiley Methodist Church. Organized, 1877.
Number of Members—Fourteen.
First Pastor—Rev. Daniel Tucker.
First Aid President—Mrs. Mary Holland Fears, served thirty-five years.
First W.H.M.S. President—Mrs. Ella Hill.
First W.F.M.S. President—Mrs. Dollie Thurman.
First W.S.C.S. President—Mrs. Dollie Wright.
First Church School Superintendent—Floyd Winslow, served eleven years.
The Charter Members Are: Edward Bailey and wife, Reuben Bailey and wife, James Shepherd and wife, Henriett Adkins, William Adkins, Joseph Dean and wife, Richard Willis and wife, Wyette Poindexter and wife.

CHICAGO, ILLINOIS

City or Town—Chicago, Illinois.
Name of Church—St. Mark.
When Organized—1894.
Number of Members—Eight.
First Pastor—Rev. S. C. Goosley.
First Aid President—Mrs. Nellie Bomar.
First W.H.M.S. President—Mrs. Liattah Crolley.
First W.F.M.S. President—Mrs. Elizabeth W. Jackson.
First W.S.C.S. President—Mrs. Lucille R. Wilkins.
First Sunday School Superintendent—Mr. R. E. Moore.

HISTORY OF THE LEXINGTON CONFERENCE

Number of Years He Served—Six months.
First Church School Superintendent—Mr. Richard A. Crolley.
Number of Years He Served—Forty.
Presiding Elder—Rev. E. L. Gilliam.
Number of Years He Served—Five.
Present Pastor—Rev. M. W. Clair, Jr.
Number of Years He Served—Five.
Number of Minister's Children—Two.
Names of Minister's Children—Phyllis Ann and Ethel Maxine.

PRINCETON, INDIANA

City or Town—Princeton, Indiana.
Name of Church—Calvary Methodist.
When Organized—1880.
Number of Members—Four.
First Pastor—Rev. Mason.
First Aid President—Mrs. Adams.
First W.S.C.S. President—Mrs. Mary Lou Lyles.
Present Pastor—Rev. Robert C. Wynn.
Number of Years He Served—One.
Number of Minister's Children—One.
Names of Minister's Children—Yyonne Clarice Wynn.

Delegates to the General and Jurisdictional Conferences

1872—NEW YORK CITY, N. Y.
    Ministerial: W. L. Muir.
    Reserve: Scott Ward.
    Lay Delegate: Marshall W. Taylor.
    Reserve: Jefferson Porter.

1876—BALTIMORE, MD.
    Ministerial: W. L. Muir.
    Reserve: E. W. S. Hammond.
    Lay Delegate: George A. Sissle.

1880—CINCINNATI, OHIO
    Ministerial: E. W. S. Hammond.
    Reserve: Scott Ward.
    Lay Delegate: C. R. Mack.
    Reserve: W. H. Talbott.

1884—PHILADELPHIA, PA.
    Ministerial: Marshall W. Taylor, Joseph Courtney.
    Reserves: E. W. S. Hammond, Daniel Jones.
    Lay Delegates: Thomas R. Fletcher, W. M. Spear.
    Reserves: L. W. Miles, C. H. Taylor.

1888—NEW YORK CITY, N. Y.
    Ministerial: Daniel Jones, E. W. S. Hammond.
    Reserves: H. W. Tate, George A. Sissle.
    Lay Delegates: Thomas R. Fletcher, George Knox.
    Reserves: W. H. Carr, R. L. Dickerson.

1892—OMAHA, NEB.
    Ministerial: L. M. Hagood, E. W. S. Hammond.
    Reserves: W. S. Rollins, W. W. Locke.
    Lay Delegates: J. M. Peters, George L. Knox.
    Reserves: G. W. Nelson, J. T. Leggett.

1896—CLEVELAND, OHIO
    Ministerial: E. W. S. Hammond, Joseph Courtney.
    Reserves: L. M. Hagood, George Sissle.
    Lay Delegates: Isaac McCullough, R. F. Broaddus.
    Reserves: Louis Robinson, Charlotte Edison.

1900—CHICAGO, ILL.
    Ministerial: Edward L. Gilliam, Elam A. White.
    Reserves: S. G. Turner, D. E. Skelton.
    Lay Delegates: B. J. Morgan, J. A. Washington.
    Reserves: B. H. Garrett, A. V. Meeks.

1904—LOS ANGELES, CALIF.
    Ministerial: Elam A. White, Joseph Courtney.
    Reserves: J. H. Stanley, L. M. Hagood.
    Lay Delegates: J. A. Washington, J. W. Mebane.
    Reserves: E. S. Foreman, R. B. Scott.

HISTORY OF THE LEXINGTON CONFERENCE

1908—BALTIMORE, MD.
Ministerial: Elam A. White, D. E. Skelton.
Reserves: E. L. Gilliam, R. L. Dickerson.
Lay Delegates: Richard A. Crolley, J. W. Mebane.
Reserves: W. J. Langston, J. A. Washington.

1912—MINNEAPOLIS, MINN.
Ministerial: E. L. Gilliam, D. E. Skelton, J. W. Robinson.
Reserves: E. A. White, F. D. Fielding, J. S. Bailey.
Lay Delegates: R. B. Scott, R. A. Crolley, W. J. Langston.

1916—SARATOGA, N. Y.
Ministerial: E. A. White, J. S. Bailey.
Reserves: G. R. Bryant, E. L. Gilliam.
Lay Delegates: R. A. Crolley, R. B. Scott, M.D.
Reserves: William Hill, James Caroll, M.D.

1920—DES MOINES, IOWA
Ministerial: J. B. Redmond, E. A. White, D. E. Skelton.
Reserves: J. W. Robinson, G. R. Bryant, W. J. White.
Lay Delegates: L. H. Carroll, Mrs. T. J. Leggett, R. A. Crolley.
Reserves: D. A. Bethea, Miss Carrie D. Murray, Mrs. F. S. Delaney.

1924—SPRINGFIELD, MASS.
Ministerial: J. B. Redmond, E. A. White, H. M. Carroll.
Reserves: G. R. Bryant, B. F. Smith, P. T. Gorham.
Lay Delegates: Mrs. C. D. C. Mebane, Dr. J. H. Carroll, William W. Cook.
Reserves: R. A. Crolley, D. A. Bethea, H. M. Gassaway.

1928—KANSAS CITY, MO.
Ministerial: S. E. Grannum, S. H. Sweeney, N. D. Shamborguer.
Reserves: R. E. Skelton, H. M. Carroll, E. A. White.
Lay Delegates: M. H. Gassaway, J. A. Washington, D. A. Bethea.
Reserves: Mrs. C. D. C. Mebane, Mrs. F. H. Bunton, Zora B. Clark.

1932—ATLANTIC CITY, N. J.
Ministerial: B. F. Smith, Stanley E. Grannum, Frank R. Arnold.
Reserves: J. B. Redmond, S. H. Sweeney.
Lay Delegates: A. Lee Beaty, Richard A. Crolley, Robert B. Scott.
Reserves: John A. Patton, Mrs. Georgia C. Hamlet, D. A. Bethea.

1936—COLUMBUS, OHIO
Ministerial: B. F. Smith, J. B. Redmond.
Reserves: D. E. Skelton, F. R. Arnold.
Lay Delegates: R. A. Crolley, D. A. Bethea.
Reserves: J. C. Traylor, Tom Fletcher.

1940—ATLANTIC CITY, N. J.
Ministerial: B. F. Smith, M. L. Harris.
Reserves: D. E. Skelton, William H. Williams.
Lay Delegates: Dr. D. A. Bethea, John A. Patton.
Reserves: E. S. Langford, W. T. Seals.

1944—KANSAS CITY, MO.
Ministerial: R. G. Morris, M. L. Harris.
Reserves: B. F. Smith, H. M. Carroll.
Lay Delegates: Mrs. Elizabeth Langford, Mrs. Edith White.
Reserves: J. Ernest Wilkins, W. Taylor Seals.

HISTORY OF THE LEXINGTON CONFERENCE

DELEGATES TO THE JURISDICTIONAL CONFERENCE

1940—ST. LOUIS, MO.
    Ministerial: William H. Williams, D. E. Skelton.
    Reserves: Damon P. Young, Robert S. Mosby.
    Lay Delegates: Miss Elizabeth Langford, W. Taylor Seals.
    Reserves: Attorney J. Ernest Wilkins, T. R. Fletcher.

1944—KANSAS CITY, MO.
    Ministerial: B. F. Smith, H. M. Carroll.
    Reserves: W. H. Wallace, Alfred Clay.
    Lay Delegates: J. Ernest Wilkins, W. Taylor Seals.
    Reserves: J. A. Patton, J. C. Traylor.

1948—GENERAL CONFERENCE
    Ministerial: R. G. Morris, M. L. Harris.
    Lay Delegates: J. Ernest Wilkins, W. Taylor Seals, Dewey Lamkins, Edith White.

1948—JURISDICTIONAL CONFERENCE
    Ministerial: B. F. Smith, H. M. Carroll, D. P. Young, N. W. Clair.
    Lay Reserves: J. T. Current, E. Langford.

Preacher's Relief Association
ORGANIZED MARCH, 1914

President ....Joseph Courtney
First Vice-President ....F. P. Fielding
Second Vice-President ....J. T. Leggett
Third Vice-President ....E. W. S. Hammond
Recording Secretary ....H. W. Simons
Financial Secretary ....J. B. Redmond
Treasurer ....E. L. Gilliam
Trustees ....J. S. Henry, Jos. Small, G. R. Bryant, W. H. Bloomer

Ministers		Ministers' Wives.	
Alexander, C. E.	$2.00		
Allen, James	2.00	–Mrs. Allen	$1.00
Byrd, A. W.	2.00	Mrs. Byrd	1.00
Bailey, J. S.	2.00	Mrs. Bailey	1.00
Bloomer, W. H.	2.00	–Mrs. Bloomer	1.00
Courtney, Jos.	2.00	Mrs. Courtney	1.00
Carpenter, T. T.	2.00		
Carroll, H. M.	2.00		
Dickerson, R. L.	2.00	Mrs. Dickerson	1.00
Dupee, H.	2.00	–Mrs. Dupee	1.00
Fielding, F. P.	2.00	–Mrs. Fielding	1.00
Ferguson, S. H.	2.00	Mrs. Ferguson	1.00
Ferguson, T. L.	2.00	Mrs. Thos. Ferguson	1.00
Foreman, H. A.	2.00		
Fisher, Paris	2.00	–Mrs. Fisher	1.00
Gilliam, E. L.	2.00	–Mrs. Gilliam	1.00
Gorham, P. T.	2.00	Mrs. Gorham	1.00
L. M. Hagood	2.00		
Hinton, H. G.	2.00	–Mrs. Hinton	1.00
Hammond, E. W. S.	2.00		
Harris, George W.	2.00		
Henry, J. S.	2.00	Mrs. Henry	1.00
Hinton, W. A.	2.00	Mrs. Hinton	1.00
–Jones, Charles	2.00	–Mrs. Jones	1.00
–Johnson, M. S.	2.00	Mrs. Johnson	1.00
Lewis, E. R.	1.00		
Lawrence, E. D.	2.00	–Mrs. Lawrence	1.00
Leggett, J. T.	2.00	–Mrs. Leggett	1.00
Love, J. H.	2.00	–Mrs. Love	1.00
		–Mrs. E. D. Miller	1.00
McCoomer, J. H. W.	4.00	–Mrs. McCommer	1.00
Perkins, Joel	2.00	–Mrs. Perkins	1.00
		–Mrs. Powell	1.00
Redmond, J. B.	2.00	Mrs. Redmond	1.00
Robinson, F. P.	2.00	–Mrs. Robinson	1.00
Robinson, J. W.	2.00	–Mrs. Robinson	1.00
Rollins, W. S.	2.00	–Mrs. Rollins	1.00
Riley, W. H.	2.00	Mrs. Riley	1.00
Robinson, Louis	2.00		
		–Anna Stanley	
Staples, G. W.	2.00	–Mrs. Staples	1.00
Singleton, Wesley	2.00	Mrs. Singleton	1.00
Simmons, H. W.	2.00		

HISTORY OF THE LEXINGTON CONFERENCE

Ministers		*Ministers' Wives.*	
Small, Jos.	2.00	–Mrs. Small	1.00
Stone, S. S.	2.00	–Mrs. Stone	1.00
Statesman, W. C.	2.00	–Mrs. Statesman	2.00
Skelton, D. E.	2.00	Mrs. Skelton	1.00
Strider, B. J.	2.00	–Mrs. Strider	1.00
Tate, H. W.	2.00	Mrs. Tate	1.00
Turner, S. G.	2.00	–Mrs. Turner	1.00
White, E. A.	2.00	–Mrs. White	1.00
White, W. J.	1.00		
White, Fred	2.00		
Ward, B. J.	2.00	Mrs. Ward	1.00
Williams, T. F.	2.00	Mrs. Williams	1.00
		–Mrs. T. L. Wilson	1.00
		–Mrs. Zeigler	1.00

Note: The minus indicates those who have passed.

Secretaries of the Conference

DR. W. H. RILEY

Dr. W. H. Riley who served fourteen years as Secretary of the Conference did his work so well that there was never a doubt at the Conference who would be the Secretary.

After fourteen years of excellent service, to the regret of the Conference, Dr. Riley resigned as Secretary. He leaves in our memory an excellent record.

D. E. S.

Secretaries of the Lexington Conference from 1870 to 1946:

E. C. Moore—two years.
L. W. Jenkins—one year.
Dr. M. W. Taylor—five years.
Dr. E. W. S. Hammond—four years.
Dr. Joseph Courtney—2 years.
Henry W. Tate—six years.
George A. Sissle—one year.
Dr. W. L. Gilliam—four years.
Dr. E. A. White—seven years.

Dr. David E. Skelton—two years.
Dr. John W. Robinson—seven years.
Dr. Walter H. Riley—fourteen years.
S. E. Grannum—five years.
John W. Chinn—two years.
Dr. W. H. Wallace—six years.
Dr. S. P. Jenkins—seven years.
S. M. Riley—two years.

Treasurers of the Conference

of the Lexington Conference from 1870 to 1946:

C. C. Moore
M. W. Taylor
G. A. Sissle
E. C. Echols
John F. Moreland
H. W. Tate
E. L. Gilliam

E. A. White
L. E. Jordan
M. W. Clair, Jr.
John A. Patton (layman)
M. W. Clair, Jr.
M. L. Harris

Miscellaneous Items

REV. GEORGE DOWNING

REV. GEORGE DOWNING

Rev. George Downing was one of the greatest evangelists the Lexington Conference ever produced. In one of his reports to the Conference he reported 484 conversions and 718 additions to the church in one year.

Other evangelists of the Conference were: T. M. Tompkins, Isaac Mason, Felix Ross, Henry White, W. W. Locke, W. H. Vaughn, James Bouren, Moses Lewis, W. H. Pope, Marcus McCoomer, J. L. Franklin, W. D. Patton, Richard Hughes, H. M. Carroll, C. E. Ball—these men were great in their field. George Downing stands at the head of the column—Blessings to his memory.

MRS. MINERVA HARVEY

Mrs. Minerva Harvey was born in Toronto, Ontario, the second of eight children to William and Slyvia Gilliam. She was educated in the public schools of Toronto and came to the States about 1896 to make her home with her brother, the late Rev. Edward L. Gilliam, who was then pastor of Coke Chapel in Louisville, Ky.

She died in 1937 in Detroit, Mich., at the age of about seventy-five years. She joined 11th Street Methodist Church, Columbus, Ohio, about 1904. She retained her membership there until she moved to Chicago, and later to Detroit, where she joined Scott's Methodist.

HISTORY OF THE LEXINGTON CONFERENCE
DR. E. W. S. HAMMOND

Dr. E. W. S. Hammond

Dr. E. W. S. Hammond was one of the great preachers of Methodism. He was proud of the Lexington Conference and ministers and laymen were very proud of him. He was three times Presiding Elder and District Superintendent. Served one term as editor of the Southwestern *Christian Advocate;* Dean of the Biblical Department of Walden University, Nashville, Tenn. His widow and daughter live in Cincinnati, his son resides in Indianapolis, Ind.

D. E. S.

THE METHODIST CENTENNIAL

The Methodist Centennial of 1884 was held at Paris, Ky., by the Lexington Conference, celebrating one hundred years of Methodism in America.

A very fine program was rendered. Those who took part were: E. W. S. Hammond, A. McDade, N. L. Carr, J. W. Mooreland, George C. Carr, H. A. Southgate, W. L. Muir, John H. Stanley, T. T. Carpenter, Felix Ross, Marshall W. Taylor (who had been elected in May as editor of the Southwestern *Christian Advocate*).

This meeting was held at the Paris, Ky., fairground, and was quite successful, having been attended in large numbers by both races.

MINISTRY OF THE LEXINGTON CONFERENCE
From 1869 to 1945

Effective	116
Retired	10
Supernumerary	4
In school (left without appointments)	5
Supply pastors	42
Deceased ministers	189
Total ministers connected with Conference	366

HISTORY OF THE LEXINGTON CONFERENCE

In seventy-six years the ethical standard of the ministers has been commendable.

Expelled for immoral conduct	5
Reprimanded in open Conference, immoral conduct	1
Withdrew under charges	2
Expelled for leaving his charge	1
Expelled for maladministration	1
Tried for maladministration, acquitted	2
Tried for immoral conduct, acquitted	4
Total	16

The men living who have built and bought churches and parsonages since 1900:

P. T. Gorham built Simpson and parsonage at Greenville, Ky.
S. E. Grannum built Mt. Zion, Cincinnati, Ohio.
W. O. Calvest built ——————, Irvington, Ky.
J. S. Roberts, Scott, Indianapolis, and church at Winchester, Ky.
George A. Well, Princenton, Ky.
H. M. Carroll, Fulton Street, Chicago, Ill.
C. J. Johnson, church at Toledo, Ohio.
B. F. Smith bought Scott Church, Detroit, Mich.
Herman Zimmerman built church, Beloit, Wis.
Joel C. Carson, St. John, Evansville, Ind.
I. C. Smith, church, Boonville, Ind.
D. E. Skelton, church at Flemingsburg, Ky., and Frankfort, Ky., also parsonage at Chaplin, Ky.
S. W. Bankhead built Berea Church, Detroit, Mich., and Palmer Memorial Church, Detroit, Mich.
W. E. White, Mt. Pleasant, Cleveland, Ohio.
John W. Chinn, McKinley Church, Dayton, Ohio.
John W. Crook, church, New Castle, Ind.
W. H. Wallace, church, Centenary, Columbus, Ohio.

These cities are the strategic centers from which our Conference has been built.

BOWLING GREEN

(1) This was the head of the Bowling Green District from 1871 to 1924: Morgantown, Senora, Taylor Mines, Drakesberry, Litchfield, Hartford, Greenville. Later Princeton, Delaney, Smithland, Owensboro, Lewis Port, Harnered, Cloverport and Hardinsburg were added.

CLEVELAND

(2) Cory for many years was all we had in northern Ohio. The church was at 37th and Central Avenues. In 1917 Mt. Pleasant, Miles Height High had their beginning.

Dr. O'Connell was a great help toward the growth of Akron, Canton and Youngstown.

CINCINNATI

(3) Our Calvary Church was organized in Big Bucktown Northeast, later it moved to Seventh Street, then Ninth and Baymiller, then Park Street, and finally to the present site.

As early as 1873 Westwood, College Hill, Batavia and Mount Healthy were organized.

CHICAGO

(4) St. Mark, Fulton Street, Gammond Memorial, St. Matthew, 37th and Cottage Grove (South Park), now Hartzell Memorial, Miller Street, Indiana Avenue, St. Paul, Minn., Beloit, Wis., Harvey and Gary.

DETROIT

(5) Scott, Berea, Palmer Memorial, Mitchell Memorial, Eight Mile, Second Grace, Flint and Pontiac, Mich.

COVINGTON, KY.

(6) Ninth Street Church, The Falmouth, Augusta, Dover and New Park Mission was built under the influence of this church.

INDIANAPOLIS

(7) Coke now Simpson Church, N. Mission (Barnes) Greencastle, Greenfield (Saulters), Terre Haute, later Princeton.

LEXINGTON

(8) Asbury known as the Old Branch Church, Spring and Upper Street. Then St. Paul, Paris, Ky., first had its beginning in Cotton Town. Warrentown, Cadentown, Georgetown, New Providence, Winchester, Versailles.

LOUISVILLE

(9) Jones Temple (Old Jackson Street), first the Pond Church near the old Bear Wallow near Shelby Street and Chestnut, later Anchorage, Mt. Washington, LaGrange, Simpsonville (Jeffersonville Mission), Madison, North Vernon, Sulphur, Bedford, Pewee Valley, Shelbyville.

MAYSVILLE

(10) Washington, Germantown, Mayslick, Lewisburg, Flemingsburg, Pleasantville, Mt. Carmel, Tallesboro, Poplar Plains, Tilton, Sherbourne, Sharpsburg, Moorefield added later.

PARIS

(11) Cotton Church, organized in Cotton Town, now called St. Paul, in the heart of the city. Leesburg, Oxford, Boyd Lair, Corinth, North Middletown, Cynthiana, Mt. Sterling added later.

Note: As the districts were set up you will notice the shifting of the churches, yet these strategic centers held their predominance and do today.

HISTORY OF THE LEXINGTON CONFERENCE

CAPTAIN C. D. STEMLEY

Chaplain in U. S. Army, World War II, Rev. Stemley gave excellent service while in the army and returns to his former work and is now pastor of Broaddus Methodist Church, Springfield, Ohio.

The Lexington Conference furnished the following Chaplains, soldiers and W.A.C.'s in the United States Army, World War II.

Chaplains: Frank R. Arnold, Robert E. Skelton, Sr., A. D. Williams, A. R. Howard, C. D. Stemley, Julius E. Hall, John Hewett, E. L. Briggs and V. D. Elliott.

Twenty-five ministers' sons, twelve ministers' daughters served their country.

Five hundred and twenty-seven sons of our Methodist families were called to the colors. To these men and women America owes a debt of gratitude. The number of soldiers given may not be a correct statement, I am only reporting the number sent to me by the pastors.

D. E. S.

TRANSFERS

As early as 1890 our Bishop began the use of the transfer system. Our work here in the Central States was growing faster than we could prepare men for the places.

There was a debate as to the wisdom of the transfers. However, we the men in the Conference, who have grown up in it, readily admit that the men who have come to us have been assets and not liabilities. Their families and high moral character have enriched the Conference and they have contributed very much to its expansion.

These are the men now with the Conference, no longer looked upon as transfers, but as brothers beloved.

HISTORY OF THE LEXINGTON CONFERENCE

CAPTAIN ROBERT E. SKELTON

Son of Rev. and Mrs. David E. Skelton, graduated from Shortridge High School, Indianapolis, Ind.; received his Bachelor of Arts from Indiana University; M.A. from Ohio Wesleyan, Delaware, Ohio; Doctor of Divinity from Garrett Institute, Evanston, Ill.; and Doctor of Divinity from Philander Smith College, Little Rock, Ark.

He served in World War I as Top Sergeant; World War II as Chaplain with the rank of Captain. He was a member of the Conference for twenty-eight years. Pastored in Ohio, Chicago, Asbury, Lexington, Barnes, Indianapolis, thirteen years, and Rushville and St. Paul, Minn. This was his last pastorate.

He was married to Miss Cleo Holland, New Castle, Ind. He leaves a wife and four children. Of his own family, a father, mother and two sisters.

"Bob," as everyone called him, was a wonderful speaker, a great preacher, and I am sure he will live in the memory of the Conference.

W. H. WALLACE

HISTORY OF THE LEXINGTON CONFERENCE

RETIRED

D. D. Terpean, Sr.   William McMorries
          W. L. Darins

ACTIVE

Charles Brower
E. E. Crawford
R. G. Morris
M. W. Clair, Jr.
B. F. Neal
O. B. Quick
J. H. Dixon
Alfred Clay

A. R. Howard
W. H. Williams
I. R. Sumner
F. F. McCallum
J. S. Roberts
H. O. McCutchin
J. H. Ellis
S. E. Grannum (in school)

DECEASED

L. M. Hagood
J. C. Brower
George W. Strafler
K. G. Turner
J. H. Greer
S. S. Josell
P. O'Connell
R. P. Threlkeld
A. R. Martin

G. C. Taylor
C. E. Alexander
H. C. Cooper
T. S. McMorris
Fred White
J. W. Pinkney
F. H. Bunton
I. O. McEwen

TRANSFERS

R. S. Mosby—to Texas.   Dr. J. T. Burch—to Tennessee.
A. N. Anderson—to Tennessee.   J. W. Watson—to Washington.
D. D. Terpean, Jr.—to Southern California.

LOOKING INTO THE FUTURE

Since 1900 the trend of our Conference has been to the west and northwest. Our St. Mark Church in Chicago, Ill., has more members than either of our districts in Kentucky.

In 1917 we only had thirty-two members in Michigan. We now have more members there than we have in Kentucky. Consult the statistical review and look at our losses in Kentucky.

Our members are moving into the northeast and northwest. In Michigan we should go into Lansing, Jackson, Kalamazoo and Waterloo. Indiana, Fort Wayne, Logansport, Kokomo, Lafayette and Gary should be added to the Indiana District in Wisconsin Madison.

YOUNG MEN OF THE CONFERENCE

To the Young Men of the Conference My Salutation:

After fifty-seven years in the ministry without a break, I give you here my record from 1889 to 1946:

HISTORY OF THE LEXINGTON CONFERENCE

Received into the church 12,467
Conversions 4,164
Baptized adults 2,341
Baptized children 957

Of the adults, many were baptized when children. The following were brought into the Conference: B. F. Smith, W. E. White, B. H. Williams, Charles M. Lee, C. J. Johnson, Ezekiel Simmons, W. H. Wallace, C. C. Miller, H. M. Mobley, M. L. J. Bellinger, R. E. Skelton, S. P. Jenkins, Charles M. Sexton, George W. Hall, John P. Pierce, B. F. Holloway, John J. McKinney, John Hewette, Thomas L. Tindsley and Horace White, pastor of the largest Congregation Church Among Colored in U. S., in Detroit, Mich., and Pres. M. L. Harris, Philander Smith College, Little Rock, Ark. Brethren will you carry on?

CHURCH NOTES

Chicago—St. Marks, organized by Dr. E. L. Gilliam in the home of John A. Washington (layman) on Dearborn Street, with six members. Now has over 4,000 members. Present site bought by Rev. W. C. Stovall, 50th and Wabash. Present church built by Rev. J. W. Robinson. Dr. M. W. Clair is planning to build a $100,000.00 church.

* * * *

Cincinnati, Ohio—Calvary, organized in Big Bucktown. Moved to Court Street, then to old Seventh and then to Ninth and Baymiller. From that address to Park and Carlisle Avenue and now at Seventh and Smith, and is one of our great churches.

* * * *

Cleveland—Greater Cory, organized by Rev. George F. Carr in home at 37th and Cedar Street. Built a small frame church. Under Dr. George A. Sissle moved to 35th and Scovall, now St. Matthews. Greater Cory under O. B. Quick was purchased in 1946. Richard Sissle organized the graded Sunday school with four teachers, Treasurer and Secretary in Old Cory. In 1946 the school had an enrollment of 1,500 scholars and a membership of 1,800 members.

Columbus—Ohio Centenary, built by Dr. W. H. Wallace, moved from Blackberry Patch by Rev. C. E. Ball. This church became the center of Methodism in the great state of Ohio.

* * * *

Detroit—Scott. In 1917 this church had thirty-two members under the leadership of Rev. H. B. Mays and supported by the thirty-two members ably assisted by J. C. Taylor and H. C. Walker has given us a great church. Since 1917 eight churches have been added in Detroit and Michigan. Scott now has 1,500 members.

* * * *

Indianapolis—Simpson. This church was organized on 15th Street under the pastorate of Simon G. Turner. A lot was purchased at 11th and Missouri and a little church at 7th and Meridian Street was moved over to the present site, where now stands the great Simpson built by P. T. Gorham.

* * * *

Lexington—Asbury, known as the Old Branch Church on Water Street, moved to High Street when the church split, and out of it Gunn's Chapel was organized by George W. Downing. Asbury is a great church in the heart of the bluegrass.

* * * *

Louisville, Ky.—Jones Temple, known in earlier days as the Old Pond Church, organized and built near the Old Bear Wallow. They then moved to Marshall Street, then to Jackson Street where a church parsonage was built. They later moved to 6th and Walnut. Under the pastorate of Dr. D. M. Jordan they are planning to build a $100,000.00 church.

* * * *

I could mention the achievements of other churches that have done wonderful work, but not having the field history I did not wish to state anything but facts. I regret that many of the pastors did not answer the questionnaire. History is made every day but is not often compiled and published.

D. E. Skelton

THINGS TO REMEMBER

(1)

The delay in publishing the History of the Conference caused some confusion. Some of the laymen and ministers asked to have their cuts returned, and failed to return them.

(2)

It is a job to publish a book, and if the leading officers of your church and church school superintendents who have served ten years or more do not appear, it is because the pastor in 1945 and 1946 did not answer and return the questionnaire.

(3)

NOTE: All profit from the sale of the book goes to the Pension and Relief. To the retired ministers' widows and children. Not one cent comes to your humble servant. It is my contribution to my Conference.

(4)

I am indebted to Doctors B. F. Smith, P. T. Gorham and H. M. Carroll for much of the material. Also to Rev. W. H. Wallace for his assistance in helping in the publication. We have done our best. May you enjoy reading the book.

D. E. Skelton

HISTORY OF THE LEXINGTON CONFERENCE
RICHARD A. CROLLEY

Richard A. Crolley was born in Atlanta, Ga. Educated at Clark University, South Atlanta. He worked in a Methodist Book Concern for forty years—became head of Billing Department. He was superintendent of St. Mark's Sunday school for forty years and later became a Trustee in the church. He was married to Mrs. Liattah Marshall Crolley. Father of three children: Alice C. Browning, Richard Crolley and Louise Lyles. At present a library has been started at St. Mark's called Richard A. Crolley Memorial Library. I started a collection of books at Forrestville School in his memory called R. A. Crolley collection—books on or about the Negro. Mr. Crolley has two grandchildren—Barbara Browning, Candy Crolley.

RICHARD CROLLEY, JR.

HISTORY OF THE LEXINGTON CONFERENCE

CABINET FOR 1946

These brethren compose the Cabinet of 1946 who will assist Bishop E. W. Kelly in the assignments of the pastors for 1947.

Chicago District: H. M. Carroll, B.D., D.D. District Superintendent. Closing his fourth year. Brother Carroll is the little giant of the Conference. He has been faithful and worked hard.

H. M. CARROLL

Cincinnati Lexington District: W. H. Wallace, A.B., D.D. District Superintendent. Closing his fifth year. Rev. Wallace is a great preacher and has shown marked leadership. His future is very promising. Completed 1947.

W. H. WALLACE

HISTORY OF THE LEXINGTON CONFERENCE

W. H. McCallum

Columbus District: W. H. McCallum, A.B., D.D. District Superintendent. Closing his sixth year. Reverend is very positive yet kind. He wants things done and gets results. He has a bright future. Completed 1947.

Indiana District: John W. Patton, L.L.B., D.D. Reverend is closing his sixth year with wonderful success. He has brought the district forward in a fine way. His successor will find a well organized district and a fine group of pastors. May his future continue bright. Completed 1947.

D. M. Jordon

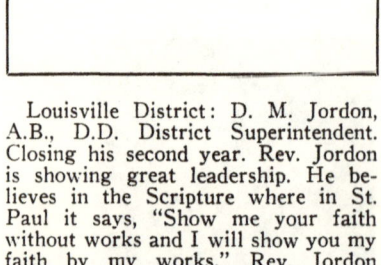

Louisville District: D. M. Jordon, A.B., D.D. District Superintendent. Closing his second year. Rev. Jordon is showing great leadership. He believes in the Scripture where in St. Paul it says, "Show me your faith without works and I will show you my faith by my works." Rev. Jordon knows his District from A to Z. We predict great things under the able leadership of this young man. Completed 1948.

CHAPLAINS IN WORLD WAR

The Lexington Conference furnished the following Chaplains, soldiers and W.A.C.'s in the United States Army, World War II.

Chaplains: Frank R. Arnold, Robert E. Skelton, Sr., A. D. Williams, A. R. Howard, C. D. Stemley, Julius E. Hall, John Hewett, E. L. Briggs and V. D. Elliott.

Twenty-five ministers' sons, twelve ministers' daughters served their country.

Five hundred and twenty-seven sons of our Methodist families were called to the colors. To these men and women America owes a debt of gratitude. The number of soldiers given may not be a correct statement, I am only reporting the number sent to me by the pastors.

D. E. S.

LOUISVILLE-EVANSVILLE DISTRICT

321 West 29th St.
Indianapolis, Ind.
January, 1937

My dear Sister:

The Director of the Women's Department of the Million Unit Fellowship movement, Mrs. J. M. Avann, has appointed me to head up this movement on the Evansville-Louisville District.

May I request that you organize your church womanhood and have a tea to be known as the International Fellowship Tea, at which time you will take a silver offering to be sent to me. I will forward what you send to Mrs. Bishop Robert E. Jones. This movement is intended to stimulate a greater interest in the Million Unit Fellowship. I am asking your women to raise $——————— and send to me by March 1, 1947. I will send the reports to Mrs. Jones. Your church will receive World's Service Voucher.

As women let us do our part. With very best wishes. I am

Sincerely yours,
Georgia M. Skelton

S:R

Dr. R. F. Broaddus

Rev. Dr. K. F. Broaddus, educated in old Berea College, entered the Conference in 1902. Member of the General Conference, 1886.

Dr. Broaddus pastored some of our largest churches. Was District Superintendent of the Louisville District six years. His greatest interest was in the Temperance cause. He spent much of his time working in the field of Temperance of the members of the Conference. I think it is only fair and just to say he was the greatest worker in the Temperance cause than any of our ministers. In his death a great leader will be missing. He leaves a wife, two sons and two daughters to carry on: Charles A. Broaddus, dentist of Trenton, N. J.; Stenson Broaddus, Manager of the Grand Theater, Louisville, Ky.; Mrs. Lavenia Yancy, clerk in the post office, Detroit, Mich.; Nettie Alice, newspaper columnist, Louisville *Defender;* Mrs. Broaddus is now manager of a Goodwill Station.

Throughout the Conference you will find both men and women who speak of how Dr. Broaddus helped them in their youth through his Temperance work.

HISTORY OF THE LEXINGTON CONFERENCE
A SKETCH OF REV. LAURA J. LANGE

Rev. Laura J. Lange

I was born at St. Matthews, Jefferson County, Ky., May 11, 1880. I attended the Jefferson County grade school through the elementary grades and thereafter attended a private school for three years.

My theological training was the prescribed three-year course at Garrett Biblical Institute, and did further study at Northwestern University. The Conference four-year course of study was taken at Philander Smith College, also one year of postgraduate work.

I was ordained a deacon by Bishop Theodore Henderson at Cincinnati, Ohio, April 18, 1926, and was ordained an elder by Bishop M. W. Clair in 1936.

I have pastored at Chaplin and Camp Branch, Eddyville and Grand River, New Haven Circuit, Smithland, Ky., Leitchfield, Ky., and New Albany, Ind., Hardinsburg and Harned, Ky.

In the years of my pastorate, one hundred and fifty-seven were brought into the church. I have married five couples. One hundred and fourteen of the above named received into the church were by conversion.

Rev. Laura J. Lange was the first colored woman to be ordained an elder in the Methodist Episcopal Church.

D. E. S.

HISTORY OF THE LEXINGTON CONFERENCE

Rev. P. T. Gorham   Mrs. P. T. Gorham

REV. P. T. GORHAM
Chicago District
3631 Calumet Avenue
Chicago 15, Illinois

January 14, 1946

Pettis T. Gorham was born seven miles from Lexington, Ky., June 28, 1866. He was reared on College Hill, Cincinnati, Ohio. He went from the high school in Cincinnati, Ohio to college, Central Tennessee College in Nashville, Tenn. He was graduated from there in 1889.

In 1897 he was graduated from Gammon Theological Seminary, Atlanta, Ga. His last work before entering the ministry was porter for the Pullman Palace Car Company.

His fiftieth marriage anniversary was celebrated in Calvary Methodist Church in 1940, just seven miles from where his wife was born and was reared from five years old. Four persons were present who were at the wedding.

His most outstanding work in the Conference was the building of Simpson Church and paying for it in Indianapolis, Ind. He paid the church and parsonage out of debt in Maysville, Ky. Put in the pipe organ in Cincinnati, Ohio. Put art glass windows in church at Paris, Ky. Paid Fulton Street Church out of debt—$3,000.00. Secured Indiana Avenue Church, Chicago, Ill. Served as District Superintendent of the Lexington District, Chicago District and the Columbus District.

HISTORY OF THE LEXINGTON CONFERENCE

The Methodist Church
NEW ORLEANS AREA
Robert N. Brooks, Resident Bishop
631 Baronne Street
New Orleans 13, La.

September 11, 1945

Dr. D. E. Skelton
321 West 29th Street
Indianapolis, Ind.
Dear Brother Skelton:

Complying with the request in your letter of August 30th, I am enclosing a biographical sketch and a mat of myself. I am sorry Mrs. Brooks does not have a cut nor photograph.

I regret that I do not have a cut the size of the sample which you enclosed. It maybe the printers can reduce the size of the mat which I am enclosing.

With best wishes to you and Mrs. Skelton, I am
Very truly yours,
Robert N. Brooks

C. T. R. Nelson

Brother C. T. R. Nelson, the Executive Secretary for the youth of The Methodist Church. He is beginning this quadrennial with marked success. Brother Nelson is a graduate from Philander Smith College and Garrett's Biblical Institute. We predict for him a great and successful future. W. H. W.

HISTORY OF THE LEXINGTON CONFERENCE
BISHOP AND MRS. A. P. CAMPHOR

BISHOP A. P. CAMPHOR   MRS. A. P. CAMPHOR

Bishop A. P. Camphor was President of Monrovia Liberia (Africa) College for fourteen years. He was elected Bishop to this field in 1916 and served this high office until his death.

Mrs. Camphor served as his faithful helpmate and both were greatly loved by the ministers of the Lexington Conference.

HISTORY OF THE LEXINGTON CONFERENCE

RICHARD A. SISSLE

Richard A. Sissle, the first Sunday School Superintendent to organize the church school under the graded system. He began with eighty-five pupils and nine officers and teachers. The Cory Methodist Church now has an enrollment of fifteen hundred students and forty-two officers and teachers.

REV. J. P. PIERCE

Entered the Conference in 1920. He is one of the little giants of the Conference. A little man who does big things. He just purchased a church at Youngstown, Ohio, at a cost of $45,-000 which a few years ago cost $80,-000 to build.

83

HISTORY OF THE LEXINGTON CONFERENCE

REV. W. E. WHITE
Came into the Conference in 1913 and has been a very successful pastor and built the first unit of Mt. Pleasant Church, Cleveland, Ohio.

REV. THOMAS H. HINES
Entered the Conference in 1933 and served six years as District Superintendent of the Louisville District, and is now pastor of our Centenary Church, Columbus, Ohio.

REV. I. D. DORSEY
Entered the Conference in 1936. He has done good work in the Conference and is now pastor of the Camphor Church, St. Paul, Minn. His is one of our best churches in the Northwest.

HISTORY OF THE LEXINGTON CONFERENCE

REV. THOMAS TINSLEY

Entered the Conference in 1937. Judging from his past record, I predict he will in time come into the leadership of the Conference.

REV. J. W. HAYWOOD, A.M.D.D.

President of Gammon Theological Seminary, Atlanta, Ga., is very much thought of by the Lexington Conference. First, quite a few of the young men of the Conference are graduates of Gammon under the guidance of Dr. Haywood. Second, he was related to the Conference by marriage, as he is the brother-in-law of our Bishop, E. W. Kelley.

MISS NETTIE ALICE BROADDUS

The daughter of Rev. and Mrs. R. F. Broaddus has been much interested in her father's work in the Temperance cause. Columnist of the largest newspaper in Kentucky, published in Louisville, Ky. Miss Broaddus also works among the youngsters of the church.

HISTORY OF THE LEXINGTON CONFERENCE

MRS. W. A. C. HUGHES

Wife of the late Bishop W. A. C. Hughes, is well known in our Conference. Bishop Hughes was much loved by the Lexington Conference. His work and aid to the Conference from the Board of Home Missions and Church Extension made him much loved by the brethren of the Conference.

MRS. BERTHA SMITH

Is one of our Conference evangelists. Very successful in revival work. Is one of whom the Conference is very proud.

S. MARION RILEY

Secretary of the Lexington Conference.

www.ingramcontent.com/pod-product-compliance
Lightning Source LLC
Chambersburg PA
CBHW060538080526
44586CB00012B/788